FOREWORD

Waheguru Ji Ka Khalsa, Waheguru Ji Ki Fateh.

The Sikh Motorcycle Club of BC needs little introduction. Started in 1999, by members who had for years been advocating for the right of Sikhs to ride with their turbans on in the province of British Columbia. Since then, they've established chapters across the globe.

As the founder of Khalsa Aid, I first learnt of them through their many fundraiser rides, supporting charities across Canada. As I write this today, they are in the news again, having just raised $113,000 for Diabetes Canada as well as riding in solidarity with the indigenous community, who are dealing with the confirmation of many unmasked graves at residential schools. Their love for riding and their love for supporting charities is unparalleled.

When I first heard of their desire to ride from Canada to Panjab and wished to do it as a fundraiser for Khalsa Aid, I was humbled. When our team tried to organize their first meeting with the club, we learnt that they were riding across Alberta, in July 2018, to celebrate the passing of laws allowing turban-wearing Sikhs to ride motorcycles. We knew then we were working with a dedicated team, that had been advocating for the turban for decades. My first meeting with the team, during a visit to Canada, was meant to be one hour and lasted several. Lots was discussed, many question asked and we knew that these were two teams that could make the ride a reality. What followed was several months of organizing that resulted in the historic world tour ride in the spring of 2019, celebrating the 550th birth anniversary of Guru Nanak Dev Ji.

Not only did the team raise a large amount for Khalsa Aid, but also touched the hearts of many across the globe. They met the Sangat in many countries, who were always so pleased to see them. Their passage through Pakistan and into India saw massive crowds. I am humbled to have met Pravjit Singh Takhar, Mandeep Singh Dhaliwal, Jatinder Singh Chauhan, Azad Singh Sidhu, Sukhvir Singh Mlait, and Jasmeet Pal Singh, the six riders who made this historic trip. Thanks also to Pravjit Singh for writing this memoir, which so honestly shows the great efforts put in to make this ride a success and the dedication of the team. Waheguru Mehar Kare.

Waheguru Ji Ka Khalsa, Waheguru Ji Ki Fateh.

Ravi Singh, CEO and Founder of Khalsa Aid Canada.

HEADING HOME
MOTORCYCLE ODYSSEY
(CANADA - PUNJAB)

Copyright © 2022 by PRAVJIT SINGH TAKHAR

All rights reserved. No part of this book may be used or reproduced in any manner whatsoever without written permission except in the case of brief quotations embodied in critical articles or reviews.

Hardcover ISBN : 978-1-7778905-1-3

Electronic ISBN : 978-1-7778905-2-0

Paperback ISBN : 978-1-7778905-3-7

For information, please direct emails to :
PravjitTakhar@gmail.com
Contact Us : +1 (778) 223-2884

TABLE OF CONTENTS

Introduction	06	April 22, 2019	109
Prepeartions	09	April 23, 2019	113
Behind the Scenes	13	April 24, 2019	117
April 3, 2019	21	April 25, 2019	121
April 4, 2019	25	April 26, 2019	125
April 5, 2019	29	April 27, 2019	129
April 6, 2019	33	April 28, 2019	133
April 7, 2019	39	April 29, 2019	139
April 8, 2019	45	April 30, 2019	143
April 9, 2019	51	May 1, 2019	149
April 10, 2019	55	May 2, 2019	155
April 11, 2019	59	May 3, 2019	161
April 12, 2019	63	May 4, 2019	165
April 13, 2019	69	May 5, 2019	169
April 14, 2019	73	May 6, 2019	173
April 15, 2019	79	May 7, 2019	177
April 16, 2019	85	May 8, 2019	183
April 17, 2019	89	May 9, 2019	187
April 18, 2019	93	May10, 2019	191
April 19, 2019	97	May 11, 2019	195
April 20, 2019	101	The Final Days	201
April 21, 2019	105	From the Author	206

INTRODUCTION

All things work together for good – a misquote to be sure, but the sentiment that comes along with that statement has significant meaning for not just myself, but for the others who contributed so much to the journey that took myself and my companions from Canada to Punjab. This quest was much more than just a fun ride on a motorcycle. The depth of commitment that we put forth, and the final result, was nothing short of remarkable on many levels, and by far, one of the proudest achievements of my life.

The best service anyone can provide is to help humanity in times of need. With a well chronicled history of doing exactly that, the Sikh Motorcycle Club of British Columbia has always been active with charity and community support. I am proud to be part of this exemplary organization, which is comprised of people from all walks of life. These people, who are united by their passion for serving the community, feeling the wind in their hair and tearing up the asphalt on their two-wheeled steeds, come from a variety of areas. The Sikh Motorcycle Club welcomes everyone and anyone who shares their passion and drive to help - not just within the local community, or within Canada, but all over the world.
My story starts with another expedition, another cause, and a simple seed planted in my imagination, from which grew a dream, and a plan.

2016
The Club had organized a charity ride from Vancouver to Quebec, using the opportunity to fundraise for the Canadian Cancer Society. While it was still in the planning stages, several of my friends and fellow riders called to ask if I would be interested in joining with them for the ride across Canada. While I thought it was quite admirable for them to be doing this for charity, the thought of riding twelve thousand kilometers on my motorcycle was daunting. I couldn't imagine the amount of time I would have to dedicate to the planning, logistics and even the financial burden that it may put on me, as I would have to take time off work and make sure that I would have the money to cover expenses for the trip. While I loved being part of the Club and working together for events and fundraisers within the community, I had never considered myself to be a hardcore rider, and this ride seemed to be a bit extreme for me, and out of my comfort zone.

So, I said no. It wasn't for me.

At the time, I had no idea that even though I didn't participate in that ride, in coming days it would have an impact on my life.

On July 10, 2016, I received a phone call from my close friend and fellow rider, Mandeep Singh Dhaliwal. He had been travelling with a group of Club members for the fundraiser between Vancouver and Montreal and had time to think about a few things as he had been riding. Without much preamble, he asked if I would be interested in planning out, and be a part of a motorcycle ride starting in Canada and ending in Punjab (India). Of course, in the moment, I thought it was a crazy proposition. It was such an outlandish idea, that I didn't even hesitate with my answer – No!

Two weeks later, I met him and the other riders as they returned to Vancouver, and he asked me yet again to consider this marathon ride. He even mapped it out a bit for me, explaining that he wanted to start a ride in Canada, travel across the ocean, and into India. My answer was still no.

The seed was sown though, in the recesses of my mind, and I couldn't let it go. I began to look at maps to see what route might be appropriate. It didn't seem possible, no matter which way I looked at it. The sheer enormity of the project scared me. There would be an inordinate amount of time needed to plan and coordinate the details of such an odyssey. I had a busy life with family and work. I couldn't dedicate time to this ambitious project.

I pushed the idea to the corner of my mind, but never really forgot about it. It was months later when I once again opened the map to see if I could figure something out that would work. Something was nagging at me to continue researching.

Would it even be possible to transport motorcycles across the ocean? Would it be feasible to drive through all of those countries? What would be required to do that? The questions plagued me and I started to dive deeper and deeper into research to find the answers.

I came across some information about travelling from Canada or Alaska to England or Europe on a cruise ship, and for the first time I wondered if there was an easy way for me to transport a motorcycle to where we would want to start the ride. After a conversation with a cruise expert though, this hope was dashed with the realization that cruise ships just don't offer that kind of service. I put the idea aside and continued with life as usual.

January 2017

A fantastic yearly motorcycle show is always held in Abbottsford, and I was eager to head over to see all the new bikes and accessories. I was surprised to see an Air Canada booth, and upon a quick conversation with the attendant, discovered that Air Canada offers the service of flying motorcycles overseas, to different destinations in Europe from Vancouver, during the months of April to September for a charge of about $1,500 CDN.

I went home and did a little more digging. The discovery that I could put my bike on a plane, the same plane that I myself could fly on, was the breakthrough I was looking for. There were four flights out of Vancouver that would carry cargo such as bikes, and with a quick phone call to Air Canada, I was able to confirm the cost. While not inexpensive, this option made a lot of sense. It was an exciting thought, but I still wasn't convinced that this was the right thing to do.

After some consideration, and keeping the information and the idea to myself for a bit longer, I decided to call Mandeep Singh and ask if this was something he really wanted to do. His resounding "Yes, Bhaji" (respectful reference to a "brother"), gave me a bit of hope. It had been more than a year since our last conversation about it, but he was hardly surprised that I was bringing up the subject again. As a good friend, he had realized that when presented with something like this, I would probably not let it go until I had figured it out.

Of course, making a voyage across the globe, on motorbikes, was not something that was going to just happen overnight. There were many plans and preparations to be made before we could consider travelling. Money and time were two challenging issues, but I was now determined to see this through. This was not going to be the first time that the club had ridden for a cause, and it wouldn't be the last. It would end up being, though, the most important ride of our lives.

PREPARATIONS

I'd lived in Canada for more than twenty years at this point and had met Mandeep Singh through the Club about five years prior. Almost annoyingly, he knew me well enough to count on me to pick up on the thread of the idea that had been presented and follow it to its end. I am certainly glad that he was persistent.

Inspiration had taken root in my mind, grown into a concrete concept and was manifesting into a potentially manageable plan. Having a background in operations management, it has always been part of my job to make sure that things operate smoothly, so once my mind was made up, I was happy to put the time in to create a successful journey. In any venture, it is imperative that everything can be managed in a way that the overall mechanics can work effortlessly.

2017 and 2018
The thoughts that were constantly running through my head were pushing me deeper into starting on the planning process, but I was still unclear on how to begin.

After a conversation with Mandeep Singh, we decided that it would be best to begin with getting a potential group of riders together. We could take the time to find likeminded people to accompany us on this trip, and, invite their ideas and potential knowledge in as we went along.

At that time, the Sikh Motorcycle Club had 125 members. It would be impossible to include every rider, so some short listing was necessary. We didn't want to have to babysit anyone along the way, in fact, we really needed those who would be helpful in all aspects. We needed companions who could work well together, but also independent enough to be able to commit to a trip of this magnitude. In the end, we created a list of ten people who we thought would be a good first group to present the idea to.
A group of that size seemed to make sense to us. A larger group could cause problems with coordination and logistics, with high odds that something may go wrong. A smaller group might pose the issue of not having enough people to support the cause and each other.

Of course, finding the right mix of personalities was a key factor. This was not a field trip or a day trip of couple hundred kilometers. The endeavour would take us across the globe, through different terrains and countries, and put us in touch with different people and cultures. Travel such as this requires someone with steady emotions, independence, grit and ability to adapt to changing situations. There was also the financial consideration. Whoever came along would need to be able to afford to invest in the expedition.

Phone calls were made and excitement started to build as our chosen few considered the proposition. We wanted to keep everything close to the vest, so we asked everyone involved not to share our plans as we worked towards finalizing everything. It would be a long process and I was concerned that once our plans were out to a larger group, an unforeseen circumstance or event might cause the plan to go awry. We also considered the fact that we thought this was something no other Canadian may have attempted and that was an incredibly exciting thought.

A meeting full of hopeful conversation was held over a fantastic dinner, and things were underway. During the subsequent discussions it came up that for some, either their families were not comfortable with them being away so long, or concerned about travel through countries such as Iran. Another dropped out because his father did not want him to go, citing that it was too dangerous. All reasons were valid, and we accepted that this kind of trip was may not be for everyone. This was an arduous ride and everyone had to come of their own free will.

In the end, there was a group of six who conceded to travel, which consisted of myself (Pravjit Singh Takhar), along with Mandeep Singh Dhaliwal, Jatinder Singh Chauhan, Azad Singh Sidhu, Sukhvir Singh Mlait, and Jasmeet Pal Singh - the youngest member of the group.

While there were some concerns about our youngest member joining us, being only twenty-seven compared to our forty-something selves, we need not have worried. Jasmeet proved himself to be reliable and confident, and eventually he fell into place within the group.

Although I was the main organizer, I really needed everyone in the group to be a contributor and on the same page for all aspects of the travel plan. I didn't want to be in a situation wherein I undertook all the prep work for the trip, only to find out later that it couldn't be done because of lack of finances. I estimated that it would probably cost each of us thirty to thirty-five thousand dollars to complete this odyssey and figured that we would probably require more than a year or so to plan the route, get the appropriate visas and anything else we needed to have finalized. Those estimates helped me conclude that we wouldn't be able to start our travel until 2019.

We agreed to open a dedicated bank account into which each member deposited a thousand dollars initially, and then five hundred dollars each month thereafter. This was a great way to ensure that everyone was contributing towards finances and it worked well for us to manage our planning expenses.

The next step was certainly a fun one – deciding which bikes we should use! Whilst it was fun, this was perhaps the most difficult challenging decision, and of course, the most expensive. It was imperative that we find appropriate bikes - ones which were reliable enough to not only make the long journey, but also be comfortable and be able to carry our belongings. They needed to be flexible enough to traverse all types of terrain and go through any type of weather we might encounter. Additionally, it was important that the bikes would not have any extreme maintenance or repair costs if there were breakdowns along the route.
We didn't want to have to deal with older bikes during our long ride, so we started researching different models, starting with BMW. We quickly discovered that they were out of our budget and too expensive to maintain or fix if something broke while travelling, so we moved on to other brands and their available options.

We eventually decided to go for the Kawasaki KLR650. An all-purpose machine with a carburetor engine that can also go off-road and is easy to modify, and does not cost an arm and leg to maintain. Before we placed the order for the bikes, we bought a used version and test drove it to Edmonton to see how it would handle. The province of Alberta had just put in place the law that Sikh riders could ride motorcycles using turbans with no helmets. Up to that point, British Columbia, Manitoba, and Ontario were the only three provinces to have that allowance in place.

The Kawasaki KLR650 passed all the necessary requirements, including being a comfortable ride up to the speed of 120 kilometers an hour, so we placed the order for the bikes and they were delivered at the end of 2018. We were in luck with our order timing, because this same model was going out of production shortly after and being replaced with a fuel-injection engine. To make them more personal, we decided to order all the bikes in yellow, a color that is of religious significance to Sikhs as it stands for sacrifice. Another benefit of the bikes being a bright color was that they could be seen more easily. The more we were seen, the safer we were.

We added modifications such as side bags, windshields, fog lights, and different navigation equipment that we knew we would need for the journey.

With these essential to-do items crossed off our list, I felt as if we were off to a good start. There was still more, a lot more, to do before departing, but every move forward meant that we were one step closer to the idea turning into reality.

BEHIND THE SCENES

The time seemed to drag by as our preparations continued. This was the only thing on my mind, even through my workdays and time with my family. I was just making the motions to take me through everyday life, with the project encompassing my free time and energy.

As I was working on the planning, there were a lot of emotions bubbling up inside me. The idea that I would be traveling to Punjab, the place where my roots are and where I was born and raised, via roadways, and for a great cause, gave me a thrill. I am proud to be a Sikh, and proud of what we as a community believe in. We recognize the human race as one, and are so blessed to be part of various cultures and societies around the world. The thoughts that swirled through my mind of my home country were many. Punjab was partitioned in 1947, and both of my parents were born in the part that is now Pakistan. My father was only two years old at the time of the partition, and his family migrated from the village of Arifwala in the original state of Punjab. Likewise, my mother was only four at that time, and her family migrated from the village of Nalewala. I wanted to see the country that was the Sikh homeland, where my grandparents and parents came from. This was a huge personal motivation that kept driving me forward.

Now, once a month, the group gathered at my house for a meeting in order to start making further progress in our planning process. Dinners would occasionally turn into five to six hours of talking and discussing ideas, routes, logistics and everything that we could think of. It was just as difficult as I thought it was going to be, but each and every member of the group pulled together for support.

No one, except for our immediate families, and those who had turned down the opportunity, knew that this plan was in the works. We had decided early on to keep it to ourselves as we made the final preparations. We spoke to each other with excitement about how our grandchildren would one day talk about what their grandparents did and the achievement that they had accomplished.

We spoke about what we would call this historic event, and eventually decided on Canada to Punjab, which spoke personally to me. While Punjab is my birth home and means the most to me, Canada has given me so much, more than I had imagined. I would never be able to pay back the country what it had given to me, as I wouldn't be where I was if I hadn't migrated to Canada. My life is owed to Canada. The name that we had dubbed our journey brought together the two countries that meant so much to me.

My family wouldn't believe me when I shared details about the trip and our plans. Their stance was that I have said a lot of things in the past but never completed the plans for them. Once our group meetings started though, my family was surprised. I was told, under no circumstances could I miss my daughter, Pearl's, university graduation, so that helped determine our travel dates. I needed to be back in Canada no later then than the end of May, as her graduation ceremony was set for June.

We decided to start our historic ride on April 3, 2019, to reach Punjab by May 11. This also worked well with Air Canada because the season in which they haul bikes as cargo started on that date. Additionally, the spring weather conditions were favourable in the cooler countries with the snow gone, and the warmer countries wouldn't be too hot. It felt fantastic to have our travel dates confirmed. Every step was taking us closer to the actual departure.

The itinerary was thought out carefully, and in the end, we decided on a slightly meandering route that would take us to twenty-two countries in total - Canada, the USA, the United Kingdom, France, Belgium, Netherlands, Germany, Switzerland, Liechtenstein, Italy, Slovenia, Austria, Slovakia, Hungary, Romania, Serbia, Bulgaria, Greece, Turkey, Iran, Pakistan, and India.

During our planning process we had deliberated extensively about what not-for-profit organization we would be supporting during this ride. This journey wasn't just for us, as we reminded each other constantly about our mission. Discussions included supporting the Canadian Cancer Society, for which the Club had previously raised one hundred and twenty-five thousand dollars. That idea was put aside as we pondered using an organization that was known and worked on a worldwide scale. We wanted an organization that people across various nations might be familiar with, but that aligned with values and mission of Sikh Motorcycle Club. For that reason, we discarded the idea of using UNICEF and several other renown global organizations. We knew that only a small percentage of their received money actually makes it to the people who needed it and there was potential that our undertaking with them may bring some bureaucratic challenges that we did not want to deal with.

I was already familiar with Khalsa Aid International, an international NGO that provides humanitarian aid in disaster areas and civil conflict zones in various places in the world. The organization is based upon the Sikh principle to "recognize the whole human race as one." We considered the fact that perhaps the Sikh communities supporting us in various countries along our route would feel more connected to the cause simply because it is associated with Sikhism and its values. The NGO was already working at the grassroots level in some of the places we were going to travel to.

Additionally, we didn't want to have to manage the money coming in for donations. We were thrilled when the CEO of Khalsa Aid came to Canada and arranged a dinner to chat about what we were doing and why we were doing it. He had set aside an hour to have dinner with us, but instead we spoke for four hours on our exciting plans and what we could do for their organization. The topic of what they could help support us with during our trip also was discussed and we were thrilled with the level of support they were willing to offer. The CEO was concerned about our safety, but I reassured him that we had considered all aspects and everything was well planned and we knew the risks.

Once everything was decided, Khalsa Aid went ahead and set up an online link, which we posted to our social media page (once we had announced the trip), with a donation button online to go directly to them. Excitingly, we could see in real-time what was being donated. It was nice for everyone to know that it was very transparent where money was going.

Supporting this not-for-profit had an unexpected benefit to us. When Air Canada found out that we were doing this ride as a fundraiser for Khalsa Aid, they discounted the transport of our bikes by a significant amount.

There were still other things to consider before our planning was finished. Having a mapped-out route meant that we could start to look at travel visas and what we needed to drive in Europe and beyond. We knew that possessing Canadian passports was going to allow us to travel quite easily through the countries in Europe, but what about places such as Pakistan, Turkey, Iran and India? These were big questions that needed to be answered before we went any farther.

I thought that getting the visa to India might be the hardest, and this was our ultimate destination, so I tackled that one first. If we didn't receive the visa to India, then proceeding with the planning of anything else would be irrelevant. With the exception of Jasmeet Pal Singh, who was in possession of an Indian passport, we all applied for ten-year visas, and waited impatiently for them to approved.

Doing more research, I discovered that most of the European countries were part of the Schengen area, which Canadian citizens do not need a visa for travel to. The exception, once again, was Jasmeet Pal Singh. He would require a Schengen visa in order to travel through those particular countries. Visa-free travel applies to stays of up to 90 days in any 180-day period, and our stays were going to be short, so it wasn't a worry for the rest of the members of the group. Romania, Serbia, Bulgaria, and Greece are not included in this area, but Canadians also do not require a visa to travel there, as long as they stay less than 90 days. I had the thought that perhaps this wasn't going to be as hard as I had originally thought. Things were starting to fall into place.

Turkey was the first country that I came across that required a paid visa to enter the country, however the online process was fast and easy, and within minutes I had downloaded copies of the visa. Pakistan, as well, required a paid visa to enter the country. We had to go in person to the Pakistan Embassy to get our visas. Surprisingly, the Ambassador greeted us at the door, provided us with some tea in his office, and after a short, friendly conversation, presented us with our visas. At that time the process took a couple of days, but now (as of January 31st, 2021) has also moved to an online system to make applying and receiving your visa even easier.

In the end, getting the Iranian visa was the most difficult. Holding a Canadian passport wouldn't help us in this case. I found that the process wasn't even straightforward, since you can't apply directly to the embassy, instead you need to hire an agent to get the visa for you. After contacting an appropriate agency, the suggestion was made that we get our Indian passports to make things easier. I am particularly proud to call myself a Canadian, and I didn't want to give up my Canadian passport, so this wasn't something that I was open to. We persisted with the idea of getting the visas with our Canadian passports. The rules were strict though, and there was potential that if the visas were denied that the entire trip could be ruined. We could only apply three months before the date that we would travel into Iran. I was worried. What if all of this planning was for nothing? With some luck, the visas worked out and we were set to travel the planned route through Iran.

While doing the research on the visas for ourselves, I came across some information about needing a type of vehicle passport for our bikes to travel through Turkey, Pakistan, Iran and India. Another dilemma. I contacted a company in the United States about something called a boomerang carnet, which they could provide, but they required a deposit of funds equivalent to the value of your vehicle. When you returned to your home country you would receive 80% of those funds back. With no other choice, we reluctantly agreed and looked at how we would pull the money together for the deposits. Upon another consultation with the company in the States, I was told that they wouldn't cover travel through Iran. More searching led to a company in England – CARS – who would cover Iran for us. A sense of relief enveloped me as I made the final deposit to them. We had our personal visas taken care of, and so did our bikes.

The important aspects of the trip were set and we were finally ready for the world to know what we had planned. The first look of the details of the trip was made public on March 19th, 2019.

We had decided to share detailed information with both print and electronic media outlets with a press conference on March 25th, 2019 in Surrey, B.C. We announced which not for profit organization we were supporting, along with the information of how people could donate and support the cause.

On the road: Six Canadian bikers will ride to Punjab promoting world peace

IP.Singh@timesgroup.com

Jalandhar: One love, one world, is what six bikers of Sikh Motorcycle Club will be promoting, as they journey through nearly 20 countries, all the way from Canada, to reach Punjab. They embark on April 3 and aim to reach Amritsar in about 40 days.

Dedicated to 550th anniversary of Guru Nanak, the bikers will also raise funds for Khalsa Aid, a Sikh NGO that is involved in relief efforts in cases of man-made or natural disasters, through their journey.

"Through this journey we want to give the message of universal humanism of first Sikh master Guru Nanak. We will be collecting donations for Khalsa Aid, which is also been following the Sikh ethos

PEACE RIDES PILLION: Sikh Motorcycle Club members

of serving people without any discrimination of region, religion, race or caste," said Pravjit Singh, one of the one six riders who will be undertaking this journey. The other five include Jartinder Singh, Azad Singh Sidhu, Zatna Dhaliwal, Sukhbir Singh and Jasmeet Singh.

The bikers are expected to pass through 20 countries. After a ride through Canada and USA, they will fly to England from where they will travel through European countries and reach Pakistan. In Pakistan, the bikers will visit different historical Sikh shrines before entering India through Wagah border to reach Darbar Sahib in Amritsar.

The club that was found in 2002, has been making quite a statement with its turbaned Sikh bikers. The club, of course, is all about safe and responsible motorcycle riding and the members are proud to proclaim to world their Sikh identity.

It was after a legal battle of 22 years by Avtar Singh Dhillon, with the support of community members, that permission to drive bikes in turbans was obtained. Dhillon loved motorcycles and also his turban and he finally managed to bring them on the same page.

Along with all the other exciting things that were happening, Sarghi Kaur Barring coordinated a promotional track for our upcoming ride, convincing Kunda Singh Dhaliwal to write it, and the well-known Punjabi singer, Nachatter Gill to sing, with music by Tejwant Kittu.

Every participant started receiving a lot of phone calls and inquiries regarding our upcoming adventure. There were a few members of the motorcycle club who were not happy to know that this trip was only for our small group. However, when we explained the expenses, hurdles, risks, and the time they would have to dedicate for this ride, they were somewhat satisfied.

We were approaching the 550th birth of the first Master of the Sikhs - Guru Nanak - which provided another motivation for us to travel, as it is a major anniversary for Sikhs around the globe. It was no surprise to see that the upcoming celebration of this event was encouraging the public to donate more than usual, as there are three main pillars of Sikh religion, which are: meditation on his name – share what you have – and, earn our living in an honest way.
Everything was falling into place and our departure date was coming quickly.

March 31st, 2019
It was a blessing to have prominent members of the community and elected government officials join us at the Gurdwara Dukh Niwaran Sahib Surrey for a pre-ride prayer gathering, along with the families of the riders and a lot of people from the general community. Everyone prayed for our safe travels and many people asked to have their picture taken with us.

I was incredulous when I realized that over $10,000 dollars had been collected at the Gurdwara Sahib by the community. It was a pleasure to be able to share that information, and the information about the donation link to Khalsa Aid with the local media who were there to cover the event.

A quick visit was also made to Guru Nanak Gursikh Gurdwara, Lynden, WA, before we returned home to finish preparing to depart the country.

APRIL 3rd, 2019
WEDNESDAY

The day was finally here! Our departure day had arrived, and we rode away from my house for a visit to Sukh Sagar Gurdwara Sahib (our house of worship), in New Westminster, before heading off to the airport to drop off our bikes at the Air Canada Cargo Terminal.

It was a hurried morning, as Jatinder Singh had to collect our Iranian visas in Washington, D.C. from the Pakistan Embassy. We had given him notarized permission to carry our passports with him in order to do this, and he had flown out the day previous, made his way directly to the Embassy, and returned on another flight. There's nothing quite like last minute chaos as you prepare to travel.

We had stopped at Gurdwara to offer prayer and seek blessings before we started on our trip. Even though the route was only about 35 kilometers from my house to the airport via Sukh Sagar Gurdwara, we were running a bit late due to waiting for Jatinder Singh. We were just leaving from our prayers when I received a phone call from Air Canada Cargo asking if we were still coming. They were waiting to get our bikes ready to fly. We were in a hurry, but we also needed to ensure that there was not more than a quarter of a tank of fuel in each of the motorcycles before we arrived at the Cargo Terminal.

Air Canada has several requirements when you ship a motorcycle with them, including that the fuel tank must be drained as far as practical; and fuel must not exceed a quarter of the tank capacity. You must ensure that batteries are installed and securely fastened in the battery holder of the vehicle and be protected in such a manner as to prevent damage and short circuits. You need to leave a spare key in the ignition and disable any alarms, radio communications equipment or navigational systems. You may leave items in your saddle bags, but an itemized list of the contents must be provided. Personal items such as clothing, toiletries and luggage cannot accompany the motorbike. Dangerous goods must be left behind.

When we arrived, the employees completed their routine checks, including going through our belongings that we had on the bikes. We had to remove the chain lubricating spray that was in our saddle bags, as it is not considered a safe item to be in the Cargo area. Other than that, everything looked good and the bikes were packed off to be loaded into the plane which would take us to our first overseas destination.

The Air Canada Cargo Terminal is conveniently located right beside the Vancouver International Airport, so once the bikes were taken care of, we went over to the main terminal to check ourselves in for our flight. Some of the members of the Sikh Motorcycle Club were at the airport to see us off for this historic motorcycle trip.

While we were completing our check-in process, we discovered that an airport employee that I knew had taken photos of our bikes being loaded into the plane, and we were extremely excited to see that the bikes were ready to go on the same flight as we were. It was even better that I was familiar with the man who had taken the pictures, as he offered to forward them to my phone. He wished us luck and mentioned that he would love to be able to do something like this someday. I was tickled to think that perhaps we were planting seeds in other people's mind for adventures and fundraisers such as this.

The destination of our flight today was London Heathrow Airport, the first international city on our itinerary. The departure was almost surreal to me, as we said our goodbyes to those who had accompanied us to the airport. All six of us were proudly wearing the special shirts that had been made to commemorate the momentous occasion. We had come together as a team for this special mission and my feelings were overwhelming. This was the start of the journey that had taken almost two years to plan, and there were so many experiences yet to come.

We boarded and took off with little fanfare, but during the flight the crew made an announcement to welcome our small group and introduce us and our cause, to the rest of the passengers. We received a $100 donation almost immediately from Mary, an elderly lady passenger. With much thanks we took the donation and were delighted that our message was being delivered to the public in so many unexpected ways. The flight crew even took a group photo with us before we got off at Heathrow London airport. We felt like celebrities!

THE TRIP WAS OFF TO AN EXCELLENT START.

APRIL 4th, 2019
THURSDAY

The flight from Vancouver to Heathrow Airport in London is approximately nine hours on a direct route and it was an easy flight. It felt as if it took a month for us to arrive, though, with the anticipation of riding our motorcycles in a different country weighing heavy upon us. The excitement was slowly building.

Arriving in the late afternoon, we gathered our luggage and headed out to the Cargo area to collect our Iron Horses. We had been concerned about the paperwork involved and required someone else to help us with it, so we roped in Jasmeet Singh's cousin, Pritpal Kaur, who was our saviour in this situation. As we got caught up in the paperwork side of things, the time flew by and we realized that it wasn't going to be possible to get the insurance we required that day. The insurance companies were already closed. Pritpal Kaur assured us that she would keep working on getting the insurance for our bikes, so we left the bikes at the terminal and the paperwork in her capable hands. Khalsa Aid helped us with the rental of a van and we departed for the city of Birmingham, a drive of approximately two hours.

While I was disappointed at the thought of leaving the bikes and starting off our tour in a rented van, it turns out that everything does happen for a reason. A sudden rainstorm hit us fiercely enroute to Birmingham. The quick drive up the M40 gave us a chance to reflect on the fact that if the insurance had worked out and we had been able to take our bikes, it would have been a hell of a ride.

While London is a booming city of approximately nine million people, Birmingham is a lot smaller, with a population of just over one million. The city, located in the West Midlands of England, has an interesting history of being an 18th century powerhouse when it came to the Industrial Revolution. Famous for several things, such as the unique Birmingham back-to-back houses and the nearby historic mining areas, the city was also incredibly well known for its manufacture of buttons, and is currently home to Cadbury World, showcasing the history of both chocolate and the Cadbury business. It was exciting to realize that we were going to spend our first night away in this lovely city.

It was incredible to see the number of people from the Birmingham community who were waiting to see us as we arrived at Guru Har Rai Sahib Gurdwara. It was a lovely opportunity to meet them and have a chance to speak with everyone about what we were doing. They all donated to our cause as well, showing the giving nature of the locals. It is hard to mention everyone that touched our hearts that day. Daya Singh Sidhu, one of the administrators at the Gurdwara, was just one of many who we spoke to and received a donation from. We enjoyed Langar (meal served in the Gurdwara) with the people who had been kind enough to come and meet us before heading off to our respective homes for the night.

I, along with Sukhvir Singh, stayed at my Massi Ji's (Massi is Mom's sister) house. In our language, we add "Ji" for anyone who is an elder and to whom we want to show respect. Jatinder Singh went to see his sister in Wolverhampton, while the others stayed at Mandeep Singh's friend's place. It was nice to see my Massi Ji, my cousins and their wives, along with my nieces and nephews, who were equally excited to see me. The family reunion was a fantastic way to spend my first night away.

This first day and night felt as if we were moving through a dream. Even after almost two years of planning, everything now seemed to be moving at light speed. I had to remind myself that this was the beauty of life. We can only wonder at the mysteries and challenges that life presents us, and only God knows what His plan is. I had never dreamed that I would be on a journey such as this, from Canada to Punjab, and certainly had never expected such an epic trip on a motorcycle for such a noble cause, and yet here I was. It was one of the happiest moments of my life, realizing that everything was falling smoothly into place. I was certain that the trip would be a success, and we would enjoy every moment.

ਗੁਰਦੁਆਰਾ ਗੁਰੂ ਹਰਿ ਰਾਇ ਸਾਹਿਬ ਜੀ
GURDWARA GURU HAR RAI SAHIB JI

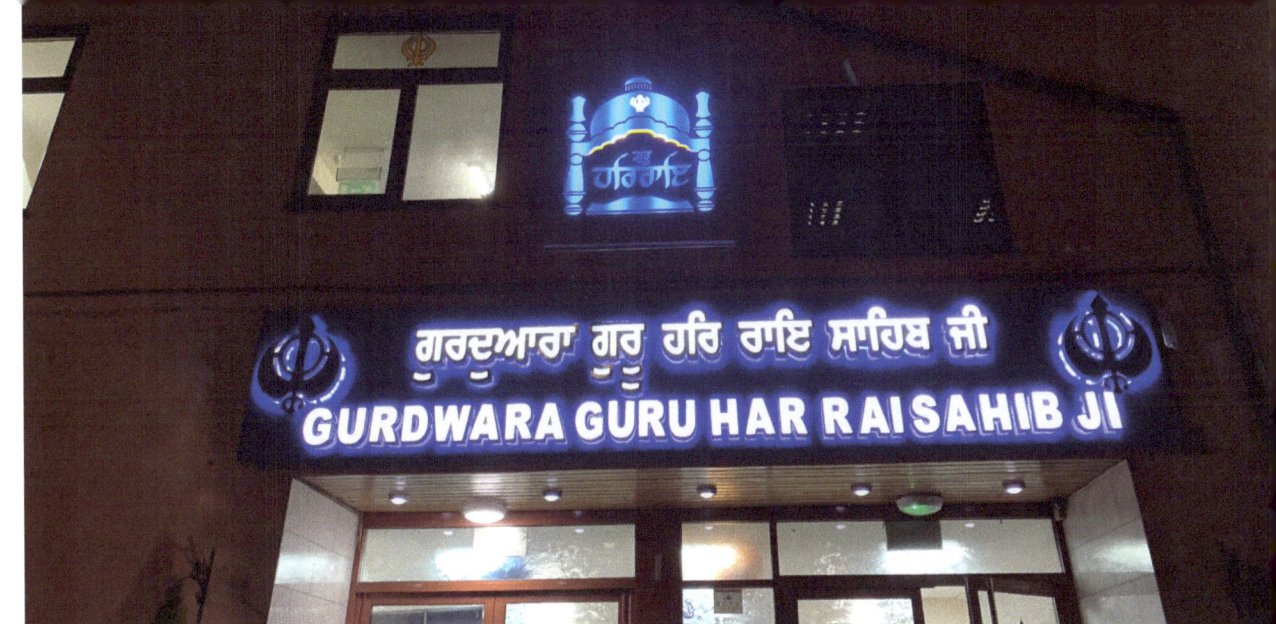

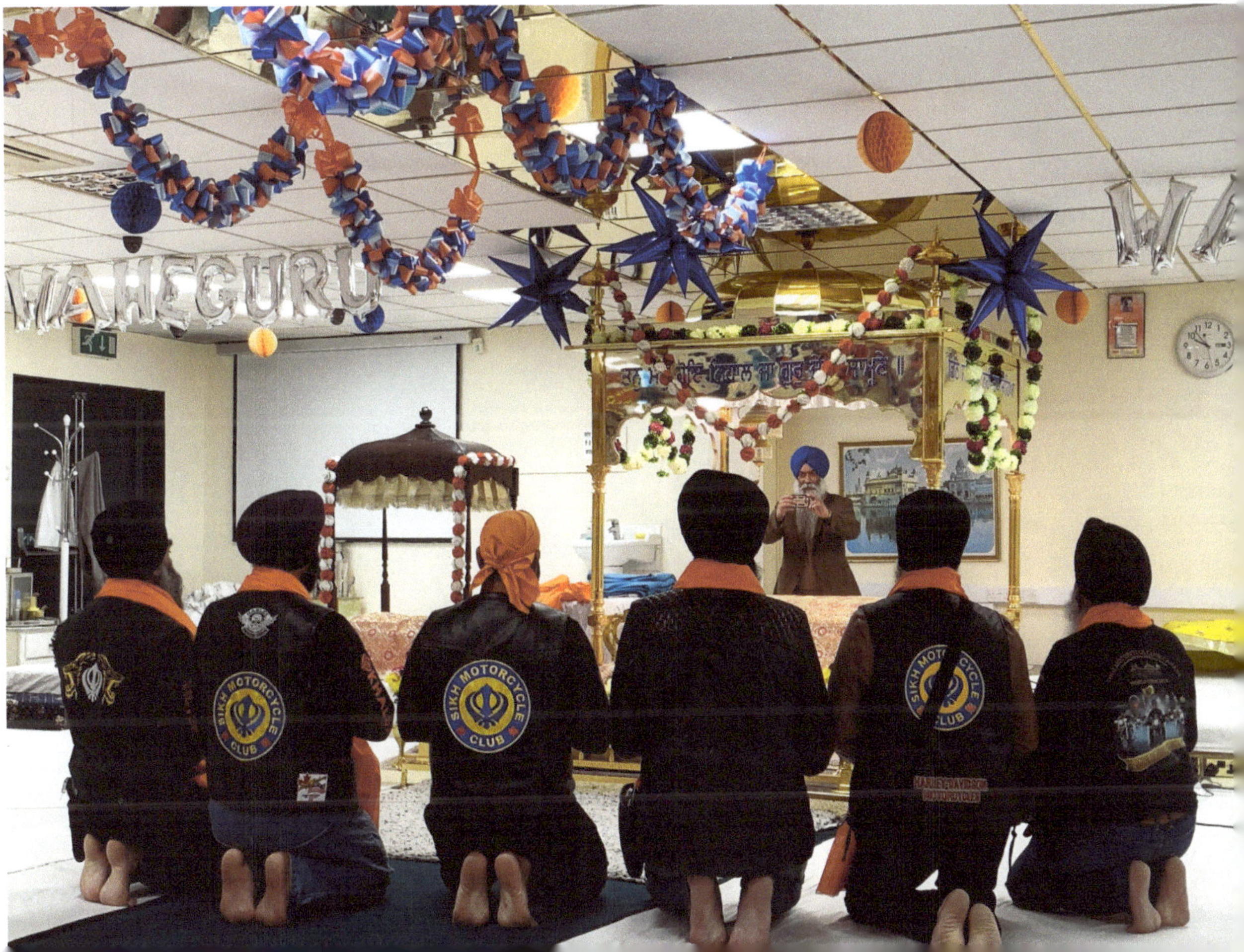
WAHEGURU
SIKH MOTORCYCLE CLUB

APRIL 5th, 2019
FRIDAY

For our first morning in England, we were treated to a typical Punjabi breakfast. Massi ji made both Sukhvir Singh and I, Aloo Parathas (Chapatis made with stuffed potatoes). It was nice to be able to share one last meal with the family before departing. They were all clamouring for photos before we left, and we happily obliged.

This was going to be a special morning for us, and we eagerly awaited Jatinder Singh's arrival. He picked us up so that we could travel in the van together to the radio and television studios in Birmingham, where we were going to share our story and mission with the local community and beyond. The news outlets were going to provide us the opportunity to get the word out to not just England, but Europe as well, and we were happy to be able to relate how the idea of the tour from Canada to Punjab began, as well as the fantastic cause that we were supporting.

It was an extremely busy day, as Khalsa Aid had set up many media interactions and interviews up for us. We had to split the group up in order to be able to attend them all. Jatinder Singh and Azad Singh went for an interview with Avtar Singh Khanda on KTV, whereas I was on a live call with Sonia at BBC Radio. It wasn't possible to say yes to everyone who wanted to interview us as our time wouldn't allow any more, which surprised me. I had already gotten used to the attention, but the sheer number of media outlets that were interested in our story was incredible. All I could think about was how epic a journey this was, not only to us, but to so many others.

We made a stop at Durga Bhawan, the Hindu Temple in Birmingham, before driving back to London. We still had to collect our bikes from the Air Canada Cargo terminal, which is located right beside Heathrow's main terminal in Hounslow. Thankfully, Air Canada didn't charge us anything extra for the overnight storage of the motorcycles, due to the nature of our ride. The insurance was in place and we were able to set off on our first ride on the other side of the road. With the day waning, we headed to where we would leave our bikes for the night, a house in Slough, just eleven miles down the road.

It was a scary ride, as we navigated the difficulty of riding on the "wrong" side of the road, along with the roundabouts, which are not common in Canada anymore. It was a strange feeling turning through the traffic circles, but we slowly mastered the art of driving on the left side as we rode along.

We had decided that we would leave the bikes in Slough, at a safe place where we knew that neither they nor our belongings that were attached to them would likely be stolen. That was a worry that none of us needed. We were spending the night at a hotel in London, which had been organized for us by Khalsa Aid. They had been most helpful in organizing some of our accommodations, as we were not sure what areas to stay in. One of the volunteers for the organization accompanied us to dinner at one of the oldest Indian restaurants in the city – called the Punjab Restaurant. It's located in Covent Garden London, and is a family owned and operated business which has been serving traditional Punjabi food since 1946. Filled with historic pictures, the atmosphere was friendly and inviting, not to mention the food was fantastic.

Covent Garden is in the heart of the West End, and is home to more than thirty-five restaurants and eating options, along with high end stores. It spreads across nine blocks and a historic piazza. This is where you will find the very best of London, and I felt privileged to be able to experience the area.

After a very enjoyable meal, we headed out to discover some of London's landmarks and sites, including the London Eye. Also known as the Millennium Wheel, the Eye is an astounding 135 meters high, and is actually the most popular tourist site in the city. While not the tallest structure to view the city from anymore (you can go higher to the 72nd floor of The Shard), the views from here are still spectacular, showcasing the Thames and the various bridges, along with the historic buildings.

We were ending a very exciting and tiring day, and while we had enjoyed every moment, we were already itching to get on the road and continue our journey.

APRIL 6th, 2019
SATURDAY

We awoke to a beautiful day and prepared ourselves for another busy morning. We enjoyed a fabulous breakfast with Ravi Singh before departing for the Khalsa Primary School in Southall. This primary school promotes and teaches children both British values and the values inherent in the Sikh faith, and this was where we were attending our UK Ride Launch Ceremony, which had been organized by Khalsa Aid International.

Our yellow riding jackets and gear stood out as we motored down the English roadways. Our jackets had the Sikh Motorcycle Club Canada's logo, along with the Khalsa Aid logo, as our name and blood type (in case of emergency), and our message of our ride to "Recognize the whole Human Race as One". We could tell, as we travelled together as a group, that we were already garnering attention.

We were slowly getting used to the riding on other side of the road and this short journey felt more natural as we swung onto the motorways and side streets. We were also getting used to riding as a small group, and it almost felt as if we were a flock of birds flying together, swaying one way and another through roundabouts and down straight lines, moving in unison as we made our way to our destination. I could only imagine what we might look like to those watching.

After seeking the blessings of Guru Granth Sahib in the open Darbar (a "hall" in a Sikh place of worship), we were fortunate enough to meet the Sangat (people gathered at Gurdwara or in the presence of the Sikh scripture called Guru Granth Sahib, which all Sikhs worship as a living Guru). We had time to share our experience so far and explain the message of our ride with the people who had joined together for this ceremony. I also met up with Grace, my high school classmate from St. Jude's Convent School, in Nakodar,

Punjab. She arrived at the ceremony with her family to wish us luck and safe travels, but also to deliver some very important papers – the travel Carnets for the motorcycles which had been issued by the British company. As there hadn't been time for them to arrive to Canada before we left, I had asked that the carnets be mailed to Grace for us to pick up. Before our time was finished at this location, we took some group and individual photos with Ravi Singh.

We said our goodbyes to everyone and left for our next stop, which was Guru Nanak Darbar, Gravesend, in northwest Kent, which is about an hour and half ride down the motorway. The astonishing architecture, along with the magnificent worship hall, the huge campus and the warm welcome by Sangat, resulted in a once in lifetime experience. This is one of the largest Gurdwara's in the United Kingdom and we could not leave the country without a visit here first.

After having langar in the Gurdwara, we continued to our ride to our hotel in Folkestone for our stay for the night. Wherever there are Sikhs, there is langar. Langar refers to meals from the free communal kitchen service that is part of every single gurdwara in the world. Through this completely voluntary service funded entirely by donations (of both food and money), Sikhs serve an estimated seven million meals a day all over the world.

The short hour ride gave us a chance to enjoy some more of the lovely English landscape and small towns before we ended our journey for the day. Also located in the county of Kent, the seaside town of Folkestone doesn't have the charming architecture or lovely sandy beaches like some of the others in the county, but instead has an interesting art scene that is growing yearly, and a fabulous variety of restaurants offering up delectable goodies of all sorts.

We had chosen to stay here for the convenient location, as the following morning we would take the nearby Eurotunnel to cross to the other side of the English Channel and enter France.

We had debated taking a ferry from the United Kingdom to get across the Channel, but we had been on ferries many times at home, crossing between the mainland of British Columbia and Vancouver Island, and had decided that the Eurotunnel would be the more fun option. As well, the ferry ride would take about an hour and a half to get across, whereas the tunnel would only take us approximately thirty-five minutes.

The Eurotunnel was officially opened in 1994 and is often referred to as the Chunnel or the Channel Tunnel. Just over 50 kilometers in length, it is the only fixed link between Great Britain and mainland Europe. A whopping 37.9 kilometers of this is under the English Channel, which means that it is the longest undersea tunnel in the world. I was surprised to learn that the idea was originally conceived back in 1802, but construction didn't start until 1988.

We were excited about the new and unique adventure that travelling the Eurotunnel would provide us, and we were looking forward to getting on the road to the next country – France.

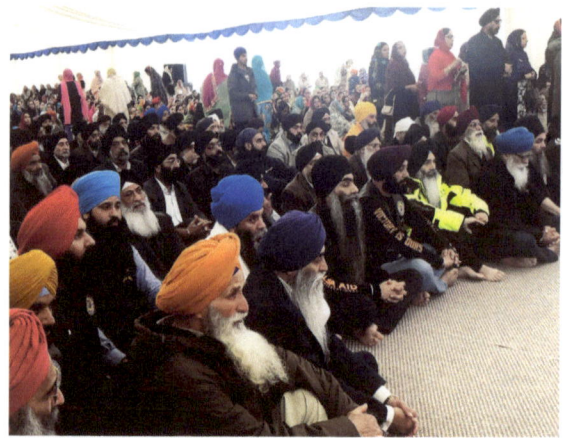

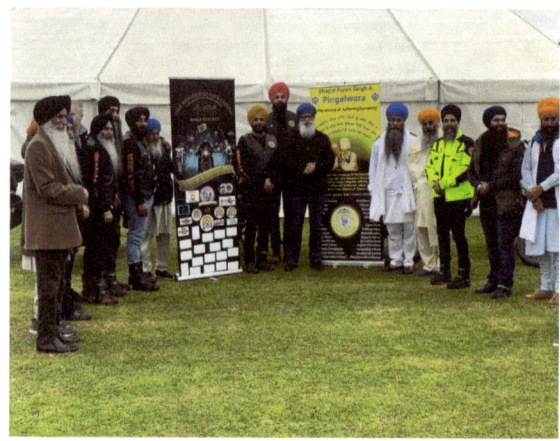

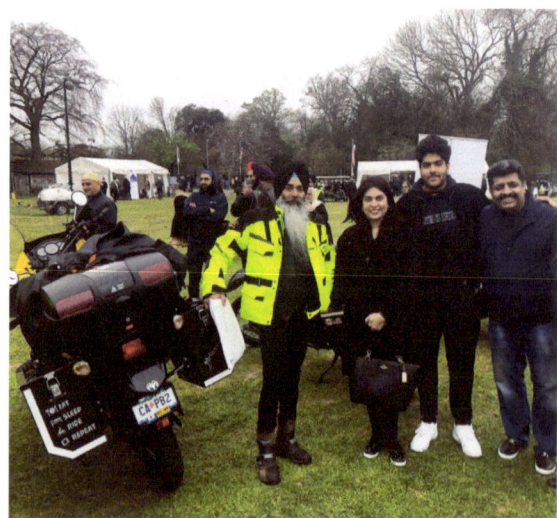

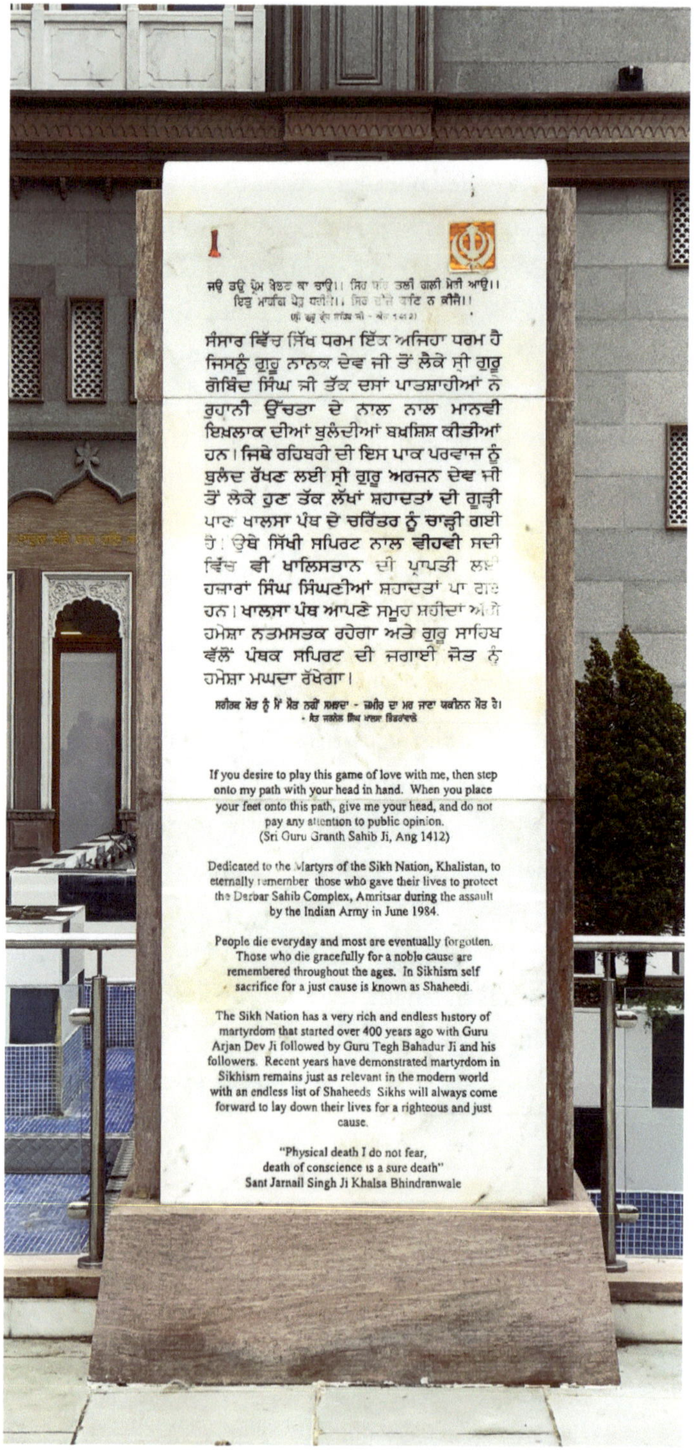
If you desire to play this game of love with me, then step onto my path with your head in hand. When you place your feet onto this path, give me your head, and do not pay any attention to public opinion.
(Sri Guru Granth Sahib Ji, Ang 1412)
Dedicated to the Martyrs of the Sikh Nation, Khalistan, to eternally remember those who gave their lives to protect the Darbar Sahib Complex, Amritsar during the assault by the Indian Army in June 1984.
People die everyday and most are eventually forgotten. Those who die gracefully for a noble cause are remembered throughout the ages. In Sikhism self sacrifice for a just cause is known as Shaheedi.
The Sikh Nation has a very rich and endless history of martyrdom that started over 400 years ago with Guru Arjan Dev Ji followed by Guru Tegh Bahadur Ji and his followers. Recent years have demonstrated martyrdom in Sikhism remains just as relevant in the modern world with an endless list of Shaheeds. Sikhs will always come forward to lay down their lives for a righteous and just cause.
"Physical death I do not fear, death of conscience is a sure death"
Sant Jarnail Singh Ji Khalsa Bhindranwale

APRIL 7th, 2019
SUNDAY

We had an extremely early start this morning as our train through the Eurochannel was departing at 6:30 am. It was still dark when we left and our visibility was severely limited due to fog, which made us very glad that it was just a five-minute drive to where we needed to check in.

This was a very exciting morning for us, as we were about to embark on the next phase of our journey – crossing over yet another international border to France. Of course, part of our excitement was due to the anticipated trip on the train, since it is the only one of its kind on the planet.

One of the fantastic things about travelling this way is that you can access immigration facilities for both Britain and France at the same, which makes the disembarkation process at the other end extremely easy. The immigration process was very smooth and the whole crew including the immigration officer and security personnel were very polite.

We were in line to board about twenty-five minutes before our departure time, and once onboard, we got off our iron horses and secured them safely on their side stands. The journey allowed us only enough time for a quick stretch of our legs and an opportunity to recheck our essentials in our saddle bags. This new way of travelling, with such a light amount of luggage, made me question if I had everything I needed, and I found myself doublechecking what I had handy. The bright, air-conditioned carriage was a nice place to spend the short thirty-five minutes.

The train brought us to the port city of Calais in France. It is well known as the "gateway to France" as the ferries and train both arrive here, along with numerous passenger vessels and other ships. Interestingly, Calais has been in the hands of not only the French, but also the British, the Spanish and the Germans at one point of time or another. While not much remains of the old fishing village that it once was, the history here is still palpable. We relished the opportunity to once again be driving on our right side of the road. In Europe, there are only a few countries that drive on the left – Cypress, Malta, and Ireland, along with the United Kingdom – so we knew from here on out we would be a lot more comfortable. The European highways are easy enough to navigate, apart from what most Canadians would consider excessive speed.

All I could think of, as we departed the Eurochannel and sped off, was how grateful I was that this was all possible. As I rode along, I thanked the Almighty for making it possible for my dream to be a reality, and in doing so, being able to contribute to a noble cause with our fundraising.

The roadway took us along the northern part of the country and into Belgium. Our destination was the gorgeous city of Ghent, where I would be meeting up with an old friend and enjoying some time promoting our ride and the purpose.

Ghent is actually the largest city in the Flanders region after Antwerp and has more historically classified buildings than any other city in Belgium. In fact, Ghent was one of the most important cities in Europe during the Dark Ages, and larger, at that time, than either Moscow or Cologne. I was a bit sad that we couldn't spend more time here, as there is so much to see and do.

Our mission was first though, and sightseeing was a far second, so we headed to our first stop of the day, which was at Gurdwara Mata Sahib Kaur, located right in the heart of the old city. It was here that I was able to meet up with an old friend that I knew from my college days in Punjab, where he had been working at the time. He had been one of the most personable employees at the college and we had stayed in contact even after I had moved away. He came, along with his brother and their families, to meet our little group, and I was very pleased to be able to catch up with him, however briefly.

We were overjoyed that the Gurdwara Sahib administrators also contributed towards the funds that we were collecting for Khalsa Aid.

After a refreshing break, with some yummy snacks and tea to help rejuvenate us, we hopped back on our bikes to head to our next stop - Gurdwara Sangat Sahib, in Sint-Truiden, Belgium. It was only an hour and a half ride from one city to the other, even though we had to circumnavigate Brussels to get there. Sint-Truiden is not a city that necessarily stands out in Belgium, but has made a name for itself in the past two centuries as a fruit growing community, as it lies in the largest fruit bearing region in Western Europe. The Abbey that dominated the city dated back to the 11th century, but unfortunately much of it was destroyed by a fire in 1975.

Upon our arrival to Gurdwara Sangat Sahib, we were impressed to see a large number of people from the local community were waiting to meet us. We happily addressed the gathering and explained the motivation behind our ride. The rest of the day seemed to fly by, as we once again spilt up to fulfill the various speaking commitments that had been arranged for us.

Our official ride of the day was over, but our personal adventures continued into the evening. We all grabbed quick showers to refresh ourselves before travelling with our host family (Tagger and Hayer family) back to the capital city of Brussels for some quick sightseeing. Of course, we could not miss seeing the incredibly beautiful La Grand Place of Brussels, also known as the Central Square in English, or Grote Markt in Dutch. This incredible square is the geographical and historical center of the city and the most visited of all places in Brussels.

The whole place was so beautifully lit up, and the architecture so stunning, it took my breath away. The buildings coated in gold are gorgeous. It is no wonder that this is considered one of the most memorable squares in Europe.

It had been a perfect day for the start of our European leg of our trip, but all days must end, and eventually we had to tuck ourselves into bed for some rest.

APRIL 8th, 2019
MONDAY

We started our day with another typical Punjabi breakfast, cooked for us by Mani Kaur. She had been instrumental in her help with Jasmeet Pal Singh's visas to travel through Europe, and we were all grateful to her. After breakfast, it only took us a short time to reload our personal items into the saddle bags and prepare to depart. We received a yummy gift of wonderful Belgium chocolate, but we were unable to take it all with us, as our space was so limited. The country is famous for its smoothly refined chocolate, and we were touched by the thoughtful gift. Belgium chocolate is well known worldwide for having a much smoother texture than others, due to their milling process. As well, the chocolate generally has a higher cocoa content than Swiss chocolates, so they tend to have a deeper flavour. Even though we had only been able to pack a little along with us, it was a nice surprise to be able to leave the country with this special present.

We took some photos with our wonderful host family before settling ourselves on our motorcycles and setting off for our next destination. We were going to be crossing two international borders today, which was an amazing thought for us, as we were used to travelling long distances within Canada to get anywhere, rather than the short distances required in Europe.

A short and pleasant forty-five-minute ride brought us to the border of the Netherlands. It came so quickly that we missed the welcome sign and had to turn around at the next exit in order to return for a picture in front of it. We had decided that this was an important part of the journey – to document our entry into each country as we travelled.

The Netherlands, also known informally as Holland, is a relatively small country, bordered to the north and west by the North Sea, to the east by Germany, and to the south by Belgium. While I knew that European countries were small, I was amazed to learn that Canada is 240 times larger than the Netherlands.

Another thirty-five kilometers down the motorway, with not even a half hour on our bikes, we came across the sign welcoming us to Deutschland (Germany). Of course, we had to pause for a couple of minutes while we captured everything on camera. As a former professional driver and a lover of motorcycles, the thought of travelling in Germany had sparked my interest right from the beginning, due to their unrestricted speed on the autobahns. The highways are created with an incredibly smooth surface, which invites speed, and the unlimited speed allowance lets drivers travel as fast as they would like to. We took advance of this opportunity and gunned the motors as we sped swiftly along.

Our ultimate destination today was the Gurdwara Sikh Center, in Frankfurt, which was only about 250 kilometers from the border of Germany, but even though we knew that we were supposed to arrive by a certain hour, it was difficult to not take our time as we enjoyed our travels and the scenery. It took us just a little over five hours to arrive to the Gurdwara Sikh Center, after thoroughly enjoying the speed, and our coffee and fuel breaks along the way.

Thankfully, they had been expecting us to be late, due to traffic and our unfamiliarity of the roadways and region. We managed to arrive in time for the evening prayer. I was incredibly thankful to see that my Aunty Palwinder Kaur was present among the local Frankfurt Sikh community members, who were waiting to welcome us.

After the prayers, we took some time for dinner and to experience the local atmosphere. We headed out to the Centrum, which is in the heart of Frankfurt, to fill up on mouth-watering pizza. The pizza place we chose to have dinner at was Luther Frankfurt, which is where my uncle Santokh Singh, and my cousin Randhir Singh work. It was really nice to have a moment to see them even if it was just for a quick visit. They weren't able to visit us where we were to be staying for the evening due to their work schedule, which was very understandable, so this was a perfect opportunity to catch up.

We soaked up the ambience of the scenic city as we savoured the evening activities, as the city is located along the banks of the river Main, which provides a pretty background. Being a hub for both business and tourism gives the city a vibe that can't really be found anywhere else, especially because it is culturally, ethnically and religiously diverse, with about half of its population having a migrant background. The history here is long, being one of the most important cities within the Holy Roman Empire, and I was itching to learn more about the story of the city, but we were short on time and I had to constantly remind myself that our priority was not sightseeing.

In the end, it was still a fabulous evening, filled with great food and company, but one particular event of that night will forever stand out in my memory. One of our riders, Azad Singh, got caught up in a conversation with a family that was dining at the same time we were. He had a lengthy discussion with them about who we were and the great cause we were riding for. To our surprise, their young child, of about eight years old, offered up his toy as a donation. The gesture almost brought tears to our eyes as we regarded this young soul who was so willing to give up something that meant so much to him. Even now, I can't imagine how touched that boy was by Azad Singh's words in order for him to give up his valued toy.

Once again, we all thanked the Lord for making it possible for us to complete this historic trip. This was an excellent example of how the understanding of the language of loving and caring for others, irrespective of colour, nationality, religion, or even language, could make such a difference in the world. One small gesture can mean so much.

The Gurdwara Administration provided us with comfortable accommodation for the night, and we went to bed thinking that we would sleep soundly with our bikes parked securely in the Gurdwara lobby. It wasn't as easy to fall asleep as I thought it would be, as the next day we were to travel into Switzerland, and the thought of riding into the country that is considered heaven on earth was exhilarating.

APRIL 9th, 2019
TUESDAY

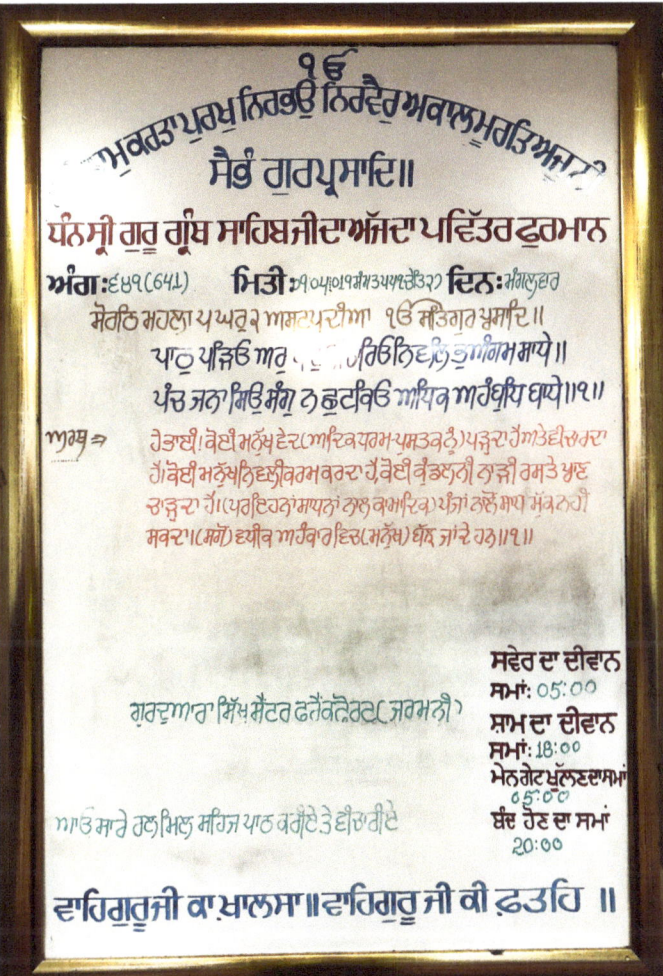

We left the Gurdwara Sikh Center in Frankfurt, while being sent off by a very heart touching kawishri. Kawishri is a traditional form of acapella folk singing, usually sung by more than one person, and they take turns singing. It is energetic and dynamic in nature and is mainly performed in religious ceremonies or during cultural get togethers, so we were extremely pleased and blessed when the community members performed for us. It was hard to say goodbye to our new friends, but there were more roads to travel and more adventures to come.

We were excited to experience the uncontrolled speed limits once again on the autobahn as we made our way through the country. Despite the high speed, the drivers here know how to move about the freeway safely, without getting in the way of other vehicles or motorcycles. We were accompanied by scattered rain showers, but with the proper gear on we continued our ride with smiles, with no intention of stopping because of the inclement weather.

The route took us alongside fields and forests, by little towns and villages. Germany has such a varied landscape depending on where you are – from forests and mountains in the central and southern regions, which are cut through by the incredible Danube, Main, and Rhine River valleys – to the wide plains in the north that reach to the North Sea.

It was taking us longer to make our way through Germany than any of the other countries we had passed through, which made sense since the country is the seventh largest in Europe. Along with bordering the North and Baltic Seas, the country shares borders with nine other European countries - Denmark to the north, Poland and the Czech Republic to the east, Austria and Switzerland to the south, and France, Luxembourg, Belgium, and the Netherlands to the west. The thought was astounding.

We wanted to get to Lörrach before the day was over, which is one of the last towns in Germany before entering Switzerland, which was about 350 kilometers from Frankfurt. Even though we knew the day was passing quickly, we were not in a big hurry to get there, as we were thoroughly enjoying ourselves.

Arriving in the early evening into Well Am Rhein, the very last town before passing through into Switzerland, we decided to partake of an excellent pizza dinner before heading off to explore anywhere else. We had chosen Milano Pizza Express Lieferservice, which was, I think, probably the best pizza I had ever tasted up to that point.

After chomping down on our delicious meal, we departed for the Rhein Center, which is the place where Germany, France and Switzerland meet, even though it was already eight thirty at night. We definitely didn't want to miss this landmark. After taking few photos to commemorate our visit, we left for the Hotel Langenthal, which was located about one hours ride from the Rhein Center in Switzerland.

Ranjit Singh, the owner of Hotel Langenthal, had contacted us prior to our trip and offered us the accommodation. He had found out that our group was on a road trip from Canada to Punjab and were doing this to raise funds for Khalsa Aid, and he wanted to support us in some way. He was waiting to welcome us upon our arrival and provided us with tasty snacks to end our day. It had been a long day, but to thank him for his generosity, we made ourselves comfortable as we chatted with him about the adventure we were on and the position of Punjabis in Switzerland.

It was well past midnight when we finally headed for our beds, but the day had been incredible, and I wouldn't have changed anything.

APRIL 10th, 2019
WEDNESDAY

It was very nice to be able to sleep in a bit this morning. I had been in a deep sleep and woken up late, as we had decided that this would be a day of no riding for us. We had been getting up very early each morning, preparing to ride, enjoying breakfasts and saying goodbye to our hosts before starting our ride, so this was a refreshing break from the routine that we had established in the short period of time that we had been travelling.

The breakfast at the hotel was just as good as what we had been enjoying with our host families previously. Ranjit Singh had arranged for us to go in two vehicles to discover the area with both himself and one of his friends driving. Sightseeing was going to be our main priority today and I was very excited to be able to view the incredible scenery and breathtaking views without having to worry about paying attention to the road.

We travelled through a plethora of twists and turns, and onto straight roadways from Langenthal to Bern. The ups and downs of the steeper sections to flatter ground was almost unbelievable, and I silently compared our own Canadian Rockies and the highways through them, to these well made and well-maintained freeways. The forty-five-minute drive flew by as we soaked in the vistas.

I was stunned by the beauty of the city of Bern's setting, as it has preserved much of its medieval character. The history of a city here dates back to the 12th century, and, even though there was a huge fire which destroyed the original wooden buildings, they were rebuilt using sandstone during the 1400's, and some of these buildings make up the historic Old Town part of the city today. This is the capital of Switzerland, and the gorgeous Federal Palace dates back to 1851.

Our time in Bern was too short, but there were more places to see and things to experience before our day was over. We headed to Interlaken, considered one of the most beautiful places in Switzerland. With postcard perfect scenery, the town itself breathes joy and the quality of life that most of us crave.

The surrounding mountainsides were covered in deep green forests, and with the resort town tucked in between the emerald-colored waters of Lake Thun and Lake Brienz, it was an almost surreal sight. The town still has old timber houses to complete the scene, and the pretty parkland on either side of the Aare River made me want to get out of the car and just stay. While we didn't have a lot of time to explore the area, we did get out to stretch our legs and take some photos which, looking back, do not do it justice. Surprisingly, I learned that this peaceful area is considered the country's adventure capital, with adrenaline junkies seeking out the rafting, canyoning, bungee jumping and sky diving that takes place here, not to mention all the hiking opportunities. I wished we had time to go off the beaten track and up into the mountains, but alas, the day still had other things calling to us. Our next stop was to seek blessings and visit the Gurdwara Sahib Switzerland. This is just one of the kinds of Gurdwara buildings in Europe, which is quite similar to Gurdwaras back home, built with a dome structure. We attended the evening prayers and spent some time with Sikhs present. It was a very pleasant way to spend part of the day.

Later in the evening, we went to the Indian Palace Indisches Restaurant to enjoy dinner. We had been invited by an acquaintance of Sukhvir Singh's, the owner of the restaurant, and who was interested in meeting up with us. The dinner was an excellent way to make new friends in the community and enjoy some conversation. Before long though, we returned to the Hotel Langenthal to catch some sleep. We were leaving for Italy the next day, and the idea of travelling into yet another country, with new things to see and new people to meet, created a palpable excitement that didn't even disperse when we went to bed.

APRIL 11ᵗʰ, 2019
THURSDAY

The late springtime beauty of the Alps took our breath away as we swept through Switzerland and on to Italy. The majestic, snow-covered mountain peaks towered above us as the serious "S" bends took us by crystal clear lakes and green pastures. The stunning vistas were only broken by the long tunnels, and with each exit into the gorgeous surrounds we were once again reminded of what a privilege it was to be making this journey. These are moments that I will never forget and the imprint of the scenery will be forever in my mind.

A short two hours after we had departed Langenthal, Switzerland, we motored across a bridge and encountered the roadway sign stating, "Welcome to Liechtenstein". Liechtenstein is, incredibly, the sixth smallest country in the world, and Europe's fourth smallest, covering an area of only sixty-two square miles. This mountainous country is the size of the city of Amritsar, half the size of the city of Surrey (British Columbia, Canada), or one-eighth the size of the city of Los Angeles. Nestled between Switzerland and Austria, it is also one of the least visited of all European countries, although, as we travel the short distance through it, we are not sure why. The air is fresh, the scenery beautiful and, with no official borders, by far the easiest country we had entered so far. A great example of independency and practicality, Liechtenstein has a population of only about 38,000 people, but the tiny country has virtually no national debt and the per capital GDP is the second highest in the world.

It certainly didn't take us long to traverse the 25-kilometre length of the country, travelling through the pretty valley. We stopped for a few minutes for some photos in the capital city of Vaduz - population of only about 5,400 residents – before continuing on our travels.

Once again, we were travelling smoothly through the Swiss countryside, having crossed back into Switzerland without any effort, enjoying every moment on our motorcycles. The feel of the motor purring under me and the wind rushing past my face gave me a sense of freedom that I wasn't sure I had experienced before. This ride meant so much to not only me, but to all of us, and each day brought us renewed joy and meaning.

Our destination today is Suzzara, Italy, which meant we had to cross another border. Entry into Italy went smoothly, and we were on our way again, with no warning of what was coming. Unexpected things can happen at any time during a road trip, and even more so when travelling by motorcycle.

As we were exiting the freeway for our very first stop in Italy, one of our group members skidded out and laid his bike down, causing quite the concern for his wellbeing. Thankfully, no major injuries were endured and the bike survived with only a few scratches to the body. The excitement was over quickly and we regained our confidence as we fueled up both the bikes and ourselves. Snacks on the side of the road in Italy somehow taste better than snacks anywhere else.

In preparation for potentially bad weather, we pulled our rainsuits on and, mounting the motorcycles again, headed off to our destination for the day – the city of Suzzara, in the Lombardy region. Italy was noticeably not the same Europe that we had been driving through previously, as we carefully navigated our way through the aggressive traffic situations and heavier traffic flow. With a whopping sixty million inhabitants, it was not surprising to see that Italy was busier, and populated areas were around every corner. We had passed the famous Lake Como and were enjoying the sites of the many towns and landscapes as our wheels spun on the pavement.

In less than a full day we had travelled from one of the least visited countries in Europe, to one of the most visited countries. It was amazing to think that while the Italian regions have so much history to them, that the country itself was only created in 1861. We could see the colorful Italian flag displayed everywhere – green for hope, white for faith, and red for charity.

We decided to bypass the large city of Milan, instead heading towards Suzzara, as the day was waning. We had travelled 450 kilometers from Vaduz, Liechtenstien, to Suzzara in approximately eight hours, with few stops for sustenance and fuel, and of course, photos.

Arriving into Suzzara, we went straight to Gurdwara Sukhmani Sahib, where we were completely overwhelmed by the Sangat gathering, especially as it was a weekday evening. After having Langar at the Gurdwara, we rode to the nearby house where we were to stay the night. It had been arranged by the Gurdwara administrators in advance for our overnight stay and a safe place to park our bikes. Another day in our itinerary was completed and I felt a deep satisfaction of what we had already accomplished as I headed to my bed and a good night's sleep.

Heading Home | 61

APRIL 12th, 2019
FRIDAY

We were treated to Chaa (tea) and Penjeri (a snack made of wheat flour, Ghee, almonds, pistachios, and cashews) before we departed for the other Gurdwara Sahib in the city - Gurdwara Singh Sabha Novellara. We were feeling fantastic as we received a lot of love and blessings from the Sangat.
The biggest surprise for us was to see Aman Singh, who we knew from Surrey, B.C. He explained that he used to live in Suzzara before he moved to Canada and that his family was still living in Italy. He introduced us to his father, and they both made us feel very at home during our time here. We were extremely thankful for their hospitality.

As well, we had to deal with more media coverage before we departed for our next destination. We were in a hurry, but I knew how important it was to connect with the local and national Italian media outlets to spread the word for our venture and cause.
While we were fulfilling our duties, it was impossible to not be impatient about getting on to our next destination. We had decided to add the beautiful city of Venice onto our itinerary, just for the sake of visiting the unique city and we were itching to get on the road.

We were excited for the drive but didn't expect what happened along the route. The roads in Italy reminded me of driving in Punjab, but with much better surfaces to ride on. The city of canals was waiting for us, and as soon as we could, our bikes were rolling down the highways towards the famous city of Venice.

During the ride, we noticed a BMW honking at us, with the driver waving at us to pull over. Concerned that something was wrong, we found an appropriate place to pull over and stopped to speak to the driver. To our surprise, the owner of the BMW was a friendly, and very respectful Sikh man named Harkamal Singh. He explained that he was from Pordenone, and was familiar with the Sikh Motorcycle Club, since it is such a unique organization and one of the first organized clubs of turbaned-wearing motorcyclists.

Harkamal Singh had learned about our little group of riders, the Canada to Punjab tour and the fundraising we were doing on social media. I was amazed. All the coverage was getting the word out, enough that a person who we had never met before had stopped us on the busy highway.
Upon learning that we were heading to Venice for some downtime, he asked if he could accompany us, and it was impossible to say no. Since he was from the area, he was familiar with where to park, so we followed him directly to the lot where visitors can leave their vehicles before entering the city.

Venice is a unique city as there are no roads for vehicles, instead tourists and locals must leave their vehicles outside the city and use the narrow pedestrian streets and canals to get around. Venice is also known as the city of bridges and the city of water, amongst other nicknames, and it was easy to see why. Built on more than one hundred tiny islands within a lagoon of the Adriatic Sea, the unmatched wealth of historic buildings and beautiful architecture caught my attention as we made our way into the city by boat.

Our local friend made sure that we saw not only the normal tourist spots, but also many that we would have missed without his guidance. As I was walking around, I felt as if I stood out among the crowds, as I was wearing my purple turban and floral bomber jacket. We stopped, at one point, to enjoy a delicious ice cream from one of the many parlors located along the narrow streets, and the treat was made even more special by the surroundings. One large courtyard that we visited was filled with hundreds of pigeons, which flew around us and even sat on our hands as we held them out. It was an unreal experience.

I noticed a strange thing about the walls of the houses as we were making our way around the fabulous city. All the walls were sitting at least two to three feet inwards from the top of the base. I figured it was probably for potential flooding but wasn't able to ask anyone to confirm that for me. We hopped into a boat taxi for a tour of the city, and I was reminded of the movie, "The Italian Job". I mentioned it to the water taxi driver, who proclaimed that he had driven one of the boats in the movie. It was an incredibly fun adventure, boating the canals around the historic city. I had been dreaming about this since I had started planning the trip, and today I was living out my dream.

It was late by the time we finished touring Venice, so we decided to say goodbye to our new local friend before heading out to where we had decided to spend the night. Our original plan was to travel a short distance to a hotel in Marghera, only ten kilometers away, but Harkamal insisted that we accompany him to his house to spend the night. We hadn't booked the hotel yet, as we hadn't been sure exactly when we would leave Venice. We couldn't refuse his generous offer, and we jumped back on our bikes to follow him to his home in Pordenone, a ride of about a hundred kilometers from where we were.

We were blessed by the chance to spend a bit more time with him in his home, and greatly enjoyed the delicious Italian pizza prepared by his wife and mother for us. The entire family welcomed us in and we spent a pleasant evening conversing and sharing life stories.

I slid off to sleep thinking about the fact that we would be leaving in the morning to travel through Slovenia towards our destination of Vienna, Austria.

APRIL 13th, 2019
SATURDAY

It was early morning as I prepared for another day on my motorcycle. The others were up and getting ready for the day as well, as our goal was to reach the city of Vienna today and we figured it would be a long day. It was going to be about 500 kilometers of riding and we wanted to reach our destination by sunset.

Our original route had not included Slovenia, but we had decided, at some point earlier, to travel through Podkoren, Slovenia, to notch another country onto our belts. It was only an additional twenty kilometers to ride through Slovenia, so we couldn't see any reason why we shouldn't. While the journey itself was long, it was no big deal to add such a short distance into our plans.

We were overwhelmed with the hospitality that Harkamal Singh and his family had shown us. I pondered on this subject as we fueled up our bodies with yummy Aloo Parontha's (Potato Stuffed Chapatis) and Lassi (Buttermilk, a typical drink in Punjab for breakfast) that we were served in the family's residence. I finally concluded that our passion for the trip, and the passion that we had for riding for a cause, not to mention the cause itself, was the backbone of the generosity that we had encountered, not just here, but in every place we had visited.

The morning sky was not visible as we departed, a light fog had enveloped everything around us, so we had dressed appropriately in our yellow riding jackets and black rain pants. I was extremely glad that I had chosen to bring along my Forma Adventure riding boots, which were proving their quality as our adventure continued.

Heading Home | 69

The ride was more than enjoyable, our wheels turning smoothly on the pavement as we made our way through the impressive Alps towards our destination. Long tunnels took us through the mountains themselves, and my eyes kept adjusting to the dark then sudden light as we zipped through the hollowed sections of the rock.

As Canadians, we are used to long road trips, and for most of us the thought of travelling only 500 kilometers is not a daunting thought, nor long in nature, but when you are riding along unfamiliar routes, with stunning vistas around every turn and interesting places to stop everywhere, a distance such as this could take all day.

Crossing into Slovenia put a smile on my face. We were entering into yet another European country, and it was amazing how easy it was to travel amongst the Schengen area's countries, as there are no border crossings. We did have to stop at the welcome sign to take our mandatory picture, of course. We had also started the habit of putting one of our club stickers on each sign as we snapped our photos. In fact, in some cases, we spent more time taking our pictures at the country's signs than in the country itself. I wished that this was a different type of trip, one in which we could enjoy each country and the uniqueness and beauty that was all around us. It was difficult to pass through these amazing places and not have enough time to explore.

We decided that Podkoren, Slovenia, was the perfect place to break for lunch, and we chose to eat at the Auto Grill to refuel and refresh ourselves. Podkoren is a charming little town that has some of the best skiing and snowboarding in the country, and plenty of outdoor activities for the summer months.

Slovenia is a surprising country, full of history, gorgeous scenery and friendly people, but also home to some of the oldest vineyards in the world, and some delectable cuisine. As well, this is a country which boasts some of the best wellness resorts in the world. Alas, there was no time for us to experience these wonders, so we continued on, trying to be satisfied with our small taste of what the country holds.

The highways and roads that pass through all these countries can have steep upgrades and downhill sections, and we encountered one of these as we continued our ride towards Vienna. The incredibly steep downhill section continued for several kilometers, which caused one of the bikes brakes to overheat. Thankfully, this was nothing serious and we knew how to rectify the problem, so we stopped at the nearest gas station for fuel and to repair what was needed.

The road was winding its way towards Austria and I was amazed at the highway infrastructure that we were seeing. The incredible bridges that provide connectivity from peak to peak were catching my attention. In some ways, Austria is much like the province of British Colombia in Canada, with greenery and beauty everywhere you turned.

It had gotten colder, and even through my heavy riding gear I could feel the change in temperature. I was sure that the temperature had dropped below zero, and I was proven correct when we finally pulled into the stunning city of Vienna and chatted with the rest of the team about it.

It had been an unforgettable day, but also long, and we were glad to arrive at the Hilton Garden Inn, right in the heart of Vienna. Once again, the Khalsa Aid team, this time the one located in Vienna itself, had been instrumental in helping us find appropriate accommodations. The underground parking meant that we didn't have to worry about our bikes overnight, and we unpacked gratefully and made our way to our rooms. It was a good opportunity to take everything out of our saddle bags to organize and repack, but at this point it was also very necessary for us to do some laundry. It seemed like the perfect time to tackle this chore, as we would have a free day in Vienna tomorrow.

It was going to be a good chance for us to reset and take care of our belongings and ourselves.

APRIL 14th, 2019
SUNDAY

It was fantastic to wake up and know that we were going to have a rest day. I had slept in, giving my body a chance to rest, so that I could stay focused and healthy for the rest of the journey. It was Sunday today, and a lovely day to spend some time meeting some new people and enjoying the city.

I decided it was also a good day to dress casually, to enjoy an easy and comfortable day. Even if we were to ride anywhere today, I didn't feel as if it were necessary to dress in my full gear. I donned the official t-shirt of the ride, and a pair of jeans and prepared myself for the day with no hurry. Our activities today were to include visits to the local Gurdwaras and seeing some of the sites that the city had to offer.

I was surprised to hear shouting from outside the hotel, and I looked down from my hotel room window to find that there was a large group of Sikh youth, all wearing Khalsa Aid shirts, shouting out the Sikh religious slogan - Bole So Nihal, Sat Shri Akal. They had arrived to accompany us through our day.

All the young Sikh boys were from the Khalsa Aid team based in Vienna. The whole team was full of energy, driving range rovers and sports cars, joking around and generally having fun. Though they were all dressed exactly as other European youths do, there were many amongst the group that were wearing turbans. The vibe was what I would have expected in urban Punjab. Languages flowed around us, fluent Punjabi and Dutch, along with others. There was a sense of pride amongst our small group as we learned that some of the youth had lived in Canada and moved overseas to be part of this volunteer organization. Their lives of Sewa Bhavna (servitude) and the spirit in which they did everything was amazing to behold.

We just had enough time to mount our bikes before the entire group pulled out in an incredible convoy, led by these young volunteers to head to the first venue - Gurdwara Teg Bahadur Sahib Ji. Here we met a lot of Sikhs who had migrated from Afghanistan. We offered prayers, followed by some snacks and tea. I felt at peace in my heart as we rode on to our next stop, which was Gurdwara Singh Sabha, where we had a chance to meet even more local Sikhs. It was such a blessing to be able to meet all of these new people and be drawn into conversations with them.

After a time, we left for our destination, Gurdwara Guru Nanak Dev Ji, which is the biggest Gurdwara Sahib in Vienna. Since it was Sunday, I wasn't surprised to see that there were a large number of Sangat present. What was surprising though, was to learn that several of them had come because they had been told that Sikh Motorcyclists would be visiting. It was still a strange sensation to think that people had come just to meet us, just as had happened in areas that we had already travelled through. I knew that Khalsa Aid International and the Sikh Motorcycle Club's social media platforms were keeping all local communities updated for our upcoming visits, but the support that we were receiving was still almost overwhelming.

It was just a coincidence that a famous Sikh preacher - Dhadi Jatha of Giani Tarlochan Singh Bhumadi - was addressing the Sikhs that particular day. Jatinder Singh had worked as a main speaker with a Dhadi Jatha in the past and recently has served in the administration of Guru Nanak Sikh Gurdwara of Surrey/Delta, so he knew Tarlochan Singh Bhumadi very well. Bhumadi Saab introduced us to the Sikhs who had gathered at Gurdwara Sahib and his group sang a couple of songs for us. As well, he shared the information of the purpose of our mission, for which we were thankful. The more we could spread the word, the better the end result would be.

There were also a lot of people at Gurdwara that day because of the Khalsa Day celebration. This is the day when the Sikh nation celebrates its birth - Vaisakhi. April 13th is when the tenth master of Sikhs, Guru Gobind Singh created Khalsa. This was the day when Sikhs were baptized for the first time and five essential beliefs were introduced.

When all of our commitments were finished, we headed back to the hotel to leave our bikes in the underground parking. Some of the local Khalsa Aid volunteers and young people wanted us to enjoy the city with them, and we were introduced to the masterpiece that is the 1st District of Vienna. This is the old city, the historic core of the city, and is found within the Ringstraße, which follows the course of the old town walls, which were torn down in the 19th century. You can see medieval history here, amongst other time periods, with the magnificent buildings and historical sites.

I felt as if I could spend hours gazing upon the scenery and still pick out new details each time I looked. Every street in this zone has a hidden gem waiting around every corner, with new things to be explored and experienced in every direction. It was an immense pleasure to just be able to walk around the city, joined by our merry group of well-wishers. As well as visiting some of the important sites, such as the beautiful St. Stephen's Cathedral, our local guides also took us to the Kahlenberg, which is a perfect viewpoint of the city, giving us the chance to see how gorgeously lit up it was in the gathering darkness. I felt sure that we would have missed some of these things if we hadn't been blessed with the people who were so eager to show us around and spend time with our little group.

Before the evening ended, the Khalsa Aid team took us out for dinner at D'Lounge, an Italian restaurant located in Millennium City (a large multipurpose building that houses retail, restaurants, offices and living spaces). We really enjoyed the company and hospitality of the group, which I found to have been the most energetic company we had during our tour so far. Our friendly and helpful accompaniers included Jodha, Romy, Inder, Mandeep, Toki, Guri, Raja, Bindi, Aman, Anmol, Harry, Deep and Gopi. Of course, there were many more people that had touched my heart during this incredible day, it would be difficult to name each and every one.

We were headed to bed with dreams of Budapest, Hungary, which was our destination for the following day.

APRIL 15th, 2019
MONDAY

We were enjoying breakfasts at the hotels before we departed each morning, which usually were complimentary, but even if they weren't, it was a convenient way to ensure that we ate before leaving. Each time we stopped on our ride, it would take us time to dismount, take off our riding gear, and then enjoy a meal, so having breakfasts in our accommodations seemed to be a good use of our time.

Our ultimate destination today was Budapest, Hungary, which was only 300 kilometers away, but we knew that we wanted to get a repair done to one of the bikes today, so we ate early and departed as soon as we could.

During a regular inspection of the motorcycles in the United Kingdom, we had noticed that one of our machines had a small cut on the side of the rear tire. We had been watching it closely, as it seemed to be a defect from the manufacturer rather than something that had happened to the tire as we were travelling. It wasn't getting any deeper or wider, but it was still a concern for us as we travelled.

We had decided that the tire should be replaced, but we hadn't had time to shop for a tire along the way. Once again, we were blessed by help from someone, this time in the form of a friend's brother. Azad Singh had reached out to Rancy Sekhon and he kindly took the information for the needed tire, purchased it and drove 300 kilometers to meet up with us in Vienna. We had gladly welcomed his company through our time in Vienna and were hugely grateful that he would go out of his way to assist us.

Now that we had the tire, we wanted to get it replaced as soon as possible. As we were soon going to be travelling into countries with much warmer weather, there was the chance that the cut would expand in the heat. That would be dangerous and not something we would want to deal with. It was much better to avoid the situation all together, so it was imperative that we reach Budapest with enough time to head to an auto shop to get that done.

Even with the idea that we wanted to arrive in Budapest early, we continued our little tradition of riding through more than one country in a day, and we were happy to have the chance to see a little of Slovakia as we rode along our route to Hungary.

Slovakia is bordered by Poland, the Ukraine, Hungary, Austria and the Czech Republic and only has about five and a half million residents. The country is mostly mountainous, which left us navigating the twists and turns of the roads, while marvelling in the beauty of the country. It was difficult sometimes to focus on the road when there was so much jaw-dropping scenery everywhere. Incredibly, although Slovakia is less than half the size of New York State, there are 180 castles and 425 châteaux here– the world's highest number of castles and châteaux per capita, and the country has 20 UNESCO World Heritage Sites. As well, Slovakia boasts more than 1,600 mineral springs, from which visitors can enjoy fresh water or a soak in mineral hot springs. It was amazing to think that all of this, and more, was available in this small country.

Of course, upon our arrival into Budapest, the first thing that we did was to take the tire and bike to RMC Motor Kft., Törökbálint, to be changed. I took the opportunity to buy a unique bandana as a souvenir, and we all got our bike chains lubricated.

We were staying in the Radisson Blue Hotel, which had been reserved for us by the local Sikhs of Budapest, but before heading to the hotel, we enjoyed a delicious lunch at the Indigo Restaurant, as we had been invited by the owner, Amandeep Singh.

With our bellies full of our fantastic lunch, we rode the short distance to the hotel to check in, park the bikes and clean up. It was another opportunity to rid ourselves of our heavy riding gear and dress casually. Our little group was quickly ready to explore Buda and Pest, as it was already late in the afternoon.

Budapest is the nation's capital, and the largest city in the country. Incredibly, this area has been populated since pre-historic times. At one time this city was called the "Queen of the Danube," as it straddles the Danube River. It consists of two parts, Buda and Pest, which are situated on opposite sides of the river and connected by a series of bridges.

We started our little tour at the Citadala, from where we could see the entire city, with the river snaking its way through it. The Parliament Building, the Riverside walk, The Palace Building and Heroes Square were other must-dos in the city. Unfortunately, we didn't have the chance to go inside any of the magnificent buildings, but it was well worth it to view the architecture and surroundings of each.

We were being shown the city by the Walia brothers and their friends, who did everything possible to make our stay in Budapest memorable. Once again, Amandeep Singh of the Indigo Restaurant arranged dinner for us, where besides having delicious flavors of Punjabi Food, we got to meet with designated personalities from the area It was incredible how many people took time out of their busy schedules to make our day in Budapest a memorable one. Expressing our gratitude didn't feel quite sufficient, and I know I will keep these people's actions and support tucked away in my heart forever.

One last stop before returning to the hotel had us savouring the colourful Hungarian sweets that were to be found at a local outdoor market. It was the perfect way to end the day. I was once again thinking of the next day as I headed to bed. We would be heading to Serbia tomorrow, another completely new experience.

APRIL 16th, 2019
TUESDAY

We took the opportunity to sleep in this morning, to restore ourselves for the coming days, but knowing that we needed to fuel our bodies before leaving this morning, we made sure that we made it down to the hotel restaurant before breakfast was over. The mouth-watering Hungarian food, including the many sweet snacks available, filled us up and prepared us for the day.

The late breakfast was followed by a return to our rooms to finish getting ready for our ride. Getting full motorcycle gear on takes more than a few minutes, but eventually we were ready to check out. We loaded our belongings on our iron horses and left the hotel, but not to head out on the highway quite yet, as we had a stop to make first. It was a gorgeous sunny day and we cruised Budapest for a while, getting the feel of the city as we rode around.

We had decided that we would like to visit the Harley Davidson store to purchase souvenirs of our journey, so that was our destination. I am a professed shopaholic, and hadn't had any time to hit the stores on this trip, so I was itching to do some shopping. Both myself and Sukhvir Singh decided to buy some flashy gloves that would glow in the dark, but this did not satisfy my craving, so I convinced the rest of the team to extend our break and spend some time shopping at the MOM Park mall before we left the city. Thankfully, Sukhvir Singh also wanted to browse the mall, so the rest of the group agreed and off we went.

We spent about an hour and a half in the mall, until our stomachs were once again growling, reminding us that we should have lunch, or at the very least some coffee to keep us going. We chose the Spiler Buda Restaurant, which was right outside the mall, with a nice outdoor patio. I gulped down a double espresso and announced that I was ready to get going, if the rest of our little troop was as well. It made us feel rich to spend the more than 4,000 Hungarian Forints on our restaurant bill, although with the exchange it was only about sixteen Canadian dollars.

It was already three in the afternoon when we finally mounted our motorcycles again to drive to Romania, which we had originally planned to pass through today on our way to Serbia, but we had made a commitment to stop in Szeged on our way, so this was our next destination. It was approximately 175 kilometers from Budapest to Szeged, a shorter ride than some of the others that we had already taken, but still very enjoyable. With a quick stop along the route for another coffee and some fuel for the bikes, we made our way towards the border.

We had been invited to have lunch at the Taj Mahal Restaurant in Szeged, by the owner, Amarjit Singh Bhullar, since this was the last town in Hungary and we had expected to be there much earlier in the day. Even though

we were quite late, we were happy to be greeted outside the restaurant by Amarjit Singh's two young daughters. The entire family welcomed us with open arms and made us feel as if we were walking into a home, rather than a restaurant. It was already six in the evening when we arrived, so instead of lunch we had a wonderful dinner followed by a typical Punjabi Chaa (tea). This is the only Indian Restaurant in the area which is owned by a Punjabi family.

It was hard to say goodbye as we hopped back on the motorcycles to continue our ride. It was already dark and we still needed to cross the Romanian border, which was one of the first in Europe where we had to complete paperwork. We watched the night sky growing darker as we completed the necessary border control papers, finally finishing and crossing into Romania at about half past eight in the evening.

It would be impossible to make it into Serbia tonight, so we booked North Star Continental Hotel in Timisoara, Romania, instead. It was located 100 kilometers from the border, and we thought we could easily ride this distance in a short period of time, but it took us almost two hours. It was the first time that we had ridden after dark, and the single lane highway, combined with the darkness and the unfamiliar route made us ride with more caution than we would have in daylight hours.

I was looking forward to seeing a bit of Romania in the daylight, as it is a beautiful country known for the forested region of Transylvania, and ringed by the gorgeous Carpathian Mountains. There are lots of castles, fortified churches and medieval towns here, including the notable clifftop Bran Castle, which has long been associated with the Dracula legend.

We thankfully headed to bed upon arrival at the hotel, with thoughts of the upcoming ride through Serbia to Bulgaria running through our minds.

APRIL 17th, 2019
WEDNESDAY

Today was a riding day. We planned to ride through to Sofia, Bulgaria today, which was a little more than 500 kilometers from where we were, which meant it would be a long day for us. We enjoyed the provided breakfast at the hotel, geared up and rumbled our iron horses onto the roadway early.

Surprisingly, by the time I was done with my regular morning prayer – Japji Sahib – which I recited while riding, we had already arrived at the Serbian border. It had taken us an hour to get here, as it was only 80 kilometers from where we had spent the night. It was a good thing we were early though, because we had to wait in line to cross the Romanian – Serbian border, and we took the opportunity to have a break from sitting on the motorcycles.

This was the first border that wasn't part of the Schengen area, so we had to spend several minutes digging through our saddle bags to find the appropriate documentation to cross. As we were organizing ourselves, an older lady came through selling fresh strawberries, which proved to be a perfect snack as we passed the time. It was interesting to see the differences between countries and traditions as we travelled. I marvelled at the uniqueness of each place and culture, and had a moment of feeling blessed pass over me as I watched the old woman selling her wares.

It wasn't too long before we were once again flying steadily down the road into Serbia, the wind in our faces. Serbia is a country at the crossroads between central and southeast Europe, and borders Hungary to the north, Romania and Bulgaria to the east, North Macedonia and Kosovo to the south, and Croatia, Bosnia and Herzegovina, and Montenegro to the west. For most of the 20th century, Serbia had been part of Yugoslavia. Belgrade, the capital, is considered to be one of the oldest and largest cities in the southeastern part of Europe. Well known for its enchanting landscapes, historical sites, fantastic cuisine and interesting culture, this was yet another country that I was sorry that we didn't have time to explore. Mentally I started making a list of all the places I would like to return to at some point in the future.

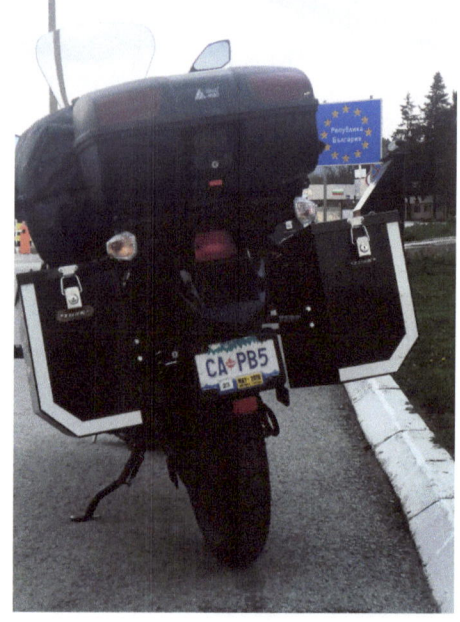

Our ride through Serbia took us about 375 kilometers, though, so we had an opportunity to see a little bit of what the country offered. The entire ride had seemed like a dream. I was feeling the grace that we had been blessed with, as everything was playing out almost exactly as we had planned. Every once in a while, I caught myself speaking out loud, asking myself if this all was really happening.

We stopped for a quick lunch, but were soon back enjoying the ride, continuing on until we saw the Bulgarian flag waving high, indicating we had arrived at the border. We were greeted with a long lineup to cross between Serbia and Bulgaria, but we had our documentation ready to hand over and passed through easily when it was our turn. With only about an hour and a half ride from the border crossing to our final destination of

Sofia, we completed the day feeling good about our timing and distance. Sofia is the capital city of Bulgaria, and is the site of more than 2,000 years of Greek, Roman, and Ottoman history, as well as marks of the more recent Soviet occupation. Most tourists miss this lovely, relaxed city as they head to the coastal areas or the ski resorts, so we were pleased to be able to spend even one night here to soak up some of the atmosphere.

We checked in at the Hotel Sofia Balkan, located on the most aristocratic boulevard in the very heart of Sofia. The Sofia Hotel Balkan was built in 1956, as part of a new architectural trend, which is a fusion of classical design and lavish décor. The iconic building of the hotel is part of the President's Palace complex and beneath its foundations lies a Roman fortress, the remains of which can be seen all around the hotel. The classical style blends in perfect harmony with the contemporary modernity of the restaurant, lobby bar and the newly refurbished guest rooms. The superb location also offers numerous restaurants as well as an easy walk to the main cultural buildings, tourist sights and shopping areas, which was perfect for our needs.

We decided to have dinner at one of the restaurants within the hotel before heading to our rooms for some rest. People who have not spent any time on motorcycles don't realize how fatiguing it is to the body to ride for long hours. As I drifted off to sleep, I had the realization that it had been two weeks since we had left home. It certainly didn't seem as if that amount of time had passed, considering our busy schedule, the fantastic places we had seen, and the incredible people we had met. It wasn't over yet, I reminded myself, there was still so much more to come.

APRIL 18th, 2019
THURSDAY

The hotel beds and rooms were so comfortable that we all had problems rising in the morning, which meant that we were the last guests in line for breakfast. It was a happy morning, and we sat around the table for some time just chatting and generally enjoying ourselves.

We had planned a ride of about 300 kilometers today, which is a relatively short distance, so we decided to take a bit of time to wander the downtown streets before departing. Of course, I wanted to do some shopping, especially for the different European style clothing that we could see locals sporting everywhere.

It had been dark when we had arrived the evening before, and there had been lots of government official's cars outside the lobby, with guards carrying heavy ammunition, so we were surprised when this morning, when we stepped out, it was as if it were a different place. It was very calm, with very little traffic coming in or out of the hotel. We explored the city streets around the hotel area, noticing lots of little shops selling liquor and sunglasses. We enjoyed stretching our legs and seeing the city for a couple of hours before we reluctantly headed back to the hotel to prepare to depart.

We returned to our rooms, got dressed in our heavy riding gear and headed down to the lobby together. We were attracting a lot of attention from other guests in the lobby, with blatant stares at our gear, facial hair and turbans. While it might have made other people uncomfortable, we were already used to the attention, as it was happening on a regular basis. My hope was that people would note the details that were on our jackets, so that they would look us up and contribute to the cause.

We repacked our saddle bags and headed out from the hotel at about noon, deliberately getting stuck in the mid-day traffic to get a bit more flavour of the city. Early on in the planning process we had decided that we would take a very quick side trip into Greece, even though we were about to leave Europe and enter into Asia, which would be the third continent on our journey. The country of Greece is someplace that beckons tourists from all over the world, as it is famous for its ancient sites and general history. It is also one of the sunniest places in the world, and has more than 6,000 islands, 18 UNESCO World Heritage Sites, about 16,000 kilometers of impressive coastline, and stunning mountains, amongst other delights. Jasmeet Singh had asked if there was any way in which we could include a visit to Santorini, Greece, during our early planning process, and I was equally excited by the prospect of visiting the famous island, but when I started to look at the logistics, I had to reluctantly say that it would not be possible. Crossing from the mainland to the island with our motorcycles would be practically impossible. We decided that was a destination that we would have to visit on our own someday.

Unfortunately, we just didn't have the time to explore the country, but wanted to be able to say that we had crossed the border, so we headed down Highway E85 off Highway A4 to enter through the Bulgarian – Greek border. There wasn't much of a wait to cross over, and we made a quick stop at the duty-free shops on the Greek side to purchase a few small items before making a U-turn and returning to Bulgaria. The border guards might have thought we were a bit crazy, but we were happy to have made this little detour.

The hotel that we had planned to stay in was located in Svilengrad, Bulgaria, just 10 kilometers from the Greek border, so we arrived within fifteen minutes. The Hotel Sahara was just one of many hotels in the town, as it is a popular place to stay. It is the last town in Bulgaria before entering Turkey. I found it interesting that, because Turkey has no casinos, that many people come to Svilengrad simply to visit the casino, which accounted for why there were so many hotels available.

The Hotel Sahara was a newly built beautiful hotel and one that I will always remember. The hospitality here was outstanding, with the most helpful and polite staff that we had encountered so far. They prepared special vegetarian meals for us and served us fresh squeezed juice that wasn't even on their menu. They had not seen Sikhs before and, finding us agreeable, took the time to ask us many questions about ourselves and our trip. The hotel was not busy, and the front desk staff sat in the lobby with us chatting. It was a pleasant way to pass the evening, and it was late evening when we excused ourselves to head up to our rooms.

As I lay in bed, I realized that we had just passed our last full day in Europe, as tomorrow we would be crossing into Turkey. I took a minute to thank the Almighty and everyone else who had made our trip successful thus far. The first phase of our ride was complete.

APRIL 19th, 2019
FRIDAY

I had slept well, and from what I could see of the rest of our little troupe, everyone else had too. It was the day that we would be leaving Europe and entering Asia, our third continent on this amazing journey. A special breakfast had been prepared for us by the staff at the hotel, knowing that we were all vegetarians. Once again, we loaded our belongings into our saddle bags, checked out of the hotel, and straddled our bikes to motor our way towards Turkey. I felt sure that the day was going to be full of wonderful discoveries and experiences.

The border of Turkey was a short 20 kilometers away from our hotel, so it didn't take us long to reach the official crossing point, in fact, only a half hour. It felt as if we had just started our ride when we arrived. When doing our planning, I had always kept in mind that it may be better to cross through borders in the mornings, rather than later in the day, so that if there were, perchance, any issues, we would have time to resolve them and still have lots of daylight left to travel in.

It was a good thing that I had thought about borders in that manner, as things here didn't go quite as we anticipated. We encountered a long lineup of vehicles and people waiting to cross into Turkey, in which we waited for three hours before our turn came up. At the checkpoint, the border authority pointed out that we didn't have the appropriate insurance on our motorcycles for entry into the country. We had purchased insurance in the United Kingdom which was supposed to cover us for all of the countries we had planned to travel through, but the officials wouldn't accept it. We decided not to argue about it and instead looked for a solution. It was fortunate that there was an opportunity to purchase right at the facility, otherwise we would have been in real trouble. It was costly – an incredible $125.00 USD per motorcycle – but we couldn't continue on without it. We had learned an expensive lesson. It wasn't worth it to purchase from another company beforehand if you are driving a vehicle into Turkey; travellers should just purchase the necessary insurance at the border as they are entering the country.

When we finally received the all clear from the authorities at the border, we rode straight through to Istanbul. The constantly changing weather patterns were making things a bit unpredictable, but the overall ride was very pleasant. Green and yellow pastures lined both sides of the highway and there were beautifully unique mosques dotted here and there consistently along the route. Spring is the best time to visit Turkey, as everything is in full bloom but the weather is not extremely hot yet.

We needed to travel a total of 300 kilometers to reach the city of Istanbul, and we were feeling the strain of the time spent at the border, along with the ride. We were feeling weary, but not tired, thankfully, when we finally reached the big city and hit the end of day traffic. The constant stream of vehicles travelling during this rush hour period really tested our patience as we spent about two hours in the huge city traversing the streets before arriving at our hotel.

It was good practice for riding in Asia, as the standard, organized lane system was evaporating before our eyes. It took a lot more concentration to drive without lanes, and I continually had to bring my focus back to the traffic streaming every which way around us. This was a common way to drive in many Asian countries, and something we would have to get used to. I tried to keep in mind that the best way to drive in another country is to always follow the mannerisms of the local drivers. We had started on the European side of Istanbul, but soon crossed the Galata Bridge which connected us to the Asian side of the city, providing us with a breathtaking ride with a night view of the city.

Turkey is in an uncommon position, as three percent of the country is considered to be in Europe, and the other ninety-seven percent is in Asia.

Our hotel for the next couple of nights was the Hotel Wyndham Grand Istanbul, and we didn't delay in checking in, as we were all tired. We retired our bikes for the night in the underground parking lot, dumped our personal items in our rooms, and departed the hotel on foot to grab something to eat and to try to soak up a bit of the city's nightlife and atmosphere. It was a nice feeling to stretch my legs after all the time on the motorcycle.

We had decided to enjoy some Greek food for our dinner, and headed to the restaurant, Big Chefs Kalamis, which was less than a kilometer away from our hotel. By the time we finally finished our meal and walked back to the hotel, it was almost midnight. It had been a very full day, and I was looking forward to tomorrow, which would be a day of rest and exploration in Istanbul. It was an incredible feeling to know that we were now in Asia.

APRIL 20th, 2019
SATURDAY

This was going to be another rest day for us, and I felt that we deserved it after our long travel the day prior. Istanbul is the magical place where East meets West, and I was excited to get out and explore, but still took the opportunity to sleep in, in fact, we all slept through the breakfast hour and awoke to discover that we needed to go searching elsewhere for our morning meal.

It was a relaxed day for which I could dress more casually again, and I was sporting an Agua blue turban, with the rest of the group in turbans of various colours. It felt wonderful to be able to get out and experience the city with no real time limits. We hopped on a ferry to East Istanbul and were rewarded during the trip by a stunning view of the coastline, along with a splendid panoramic view of the city. There were an incredible number of monuments and sites visible from the ferry, including the great palaces of Dolmabahce and Beylerbeyi, the University of Galatasaray, the Blue Mosque, the Hagia Mosque and two incredible suspension bridges.

It wasn't long after getting off the ferry that we decided to stop for brunch and Turkish tea at one of the local restaurants. Tea is big in Turkey, and it is the second most consumed beverage in the country, after water. I loved the tea here, which is more like the tea I am used to drinking, even though I had to add a bit of sugar to bring it up to the sweetness level that I craved.

Feeling rejuvenated from our brunch, we set off to view the stunning architecture of the Blue Mosque. This mosque is named the Sultan Ahmed Mosque, but well known as the Blue Mosque due to the bluish interior decorations. It is the most important mosque of Istanbul and stands next to the Byzantine Hippodrome in the old city center. It was built by the Ottoman sultan Ahmed I between 1609 – 1616, facing Hagia Sophia, in order to compete with it. A fascinating place for anyone interested in history, art or religion, it is one of the most visited sites in the city.

We were enjoying our leisurely stroll around the Blue Mosque, taking various photos and generally soaking in the atmosphere. Completely forgetting about a conversation that we had regarding posting our location on social media, I was overly excited about our location and went live on Facebook, which I don't do that often. Of course, when the rest of the team realized what I was doing, they reminded me that we had spoken about delaying our posts, with the idea that we were thinking about our safety. Quickly, I removed the live feed, apologizing profusely to my companions.

With the idea that I needed some shopping time, we wandered to the back side of the Blue Mosque where there is a small lane with shops on both sides. I was on a search for some good deals and this was such a convenient spot to try to find what I was looking for. The Arasta Bazaar proved to be a cute market area, and I decided to purchase a couple of lovely scarfs, which I found were a fraction of the price that I had seen other places. Rates of products may vary here and there in markets in Istanbul, and I was happy that we had come across one that had extremely reasonable prices for goods.

This was just a little market compared to the most famous market in Istanbul – the Grand Bazaar – which is a 550-year-old covered market. It is also one of the largest and oldest covered markets in the world. The Grand Bazaar is a series of covered passageways and corridors featuring 64 streets, 4,000 shops, 22 entrances and 25,000 employees. You can find anything from the finest silky shawls and scarves in traditional patterns to traditional items, antiques, leather goods, ceramics, the famous carpets, spices, beautiful handicrafts and gold and jewelry. Most tourists head here to purchase all sorts of goodies before returning home.

We had another place on our agenda though, so we passed up the opportunity to visit the Grand Bazaar in order to take the tunnel back to western side of the city, where the Harley Davidson Istanbul store was. Our original plan was to spend a second night in Istanbul, but as the day went by, we discussed leaving that evening instead, to avoid the crazy morning traffic. When the decision was made, we booked the Hotel Best Western Premier in Sakarya, located two hours east from the city. We quickly packed up and headed out. The drive was spectacular, giving us the feeling that we were on the Sea to Sky Highway back home in British Columbia, with the beautiful mountains on one side and the sparkling water of the sea on the other. We rejoiced in the freedom of being out the big city, as towards the end of our time there it had started to feel suffocating. I thought of another benefit as we were heading towards our hotel for the evening, and that was we would be reducing our next day's ride by about 150 kilometers.

As we travelled the two hours towards our destination, I was struck by the differences here. One thing in particular stood out for me. Every gas station that we stopped in to fill up had fresh honey to sell in little bowls. Each bowl was wrapped in plastic wrap and the honey was being sold with the comb as well. In order to enjoy the honey, you had to squeeze the honeycomb. It was a charming aspect of the countryside and I was enjoying noticing the differences between the countries as we travelled through. The world is big and every country is unique, and my eyes were being opened to all the wonderful characteristics and idiosyncrasies of each place we travelled through. We arrived safely and had the rest of the evening to relax, which was much required, because we were planning a full day tomorrow.

APRIL 21ᵗʰ, 2019
SUNDAY

It was a sunny morning when we awoke, feeling refreshed from a sound night's sleep and ready for the day. Breakfast was served at the hotel, with plenty of shots of Turkish Tea. We were slowly getting used to the taste of tea with no milk, but after a few sips without, I still found myself pouring a bit in, to satisfy my tastebuds. It is interesting how we get so set in our ways and how difficult it is to break habits, especially when it comes to taste.

During breakfast we happened to glance outside and realized that the sun had disappeared and it was now raining heavily. We quickly finished breakfast and returned to our rooms to don our rain gear, which consisted of one-piece waterproof yellow overalls. We met in the lobby and reminded ourselves with a bit of a pep talk, that with the proper rain gear the day was not lost, and that we could still ride.

We had planned to cross Turkey, starting from the north, and we kept up with our Google maps, which took us through the lovely Pontic Mountain range, which is a series of mountainous ridges. It was only two hours into our ride when the wet, stormy weather changed to snow showers. It didn't take long before we realized we were riding on wet snow that wasn't melting when it hit the ground. It was the first time that I had ever ridden my motorcycle on snow.

Everything around us was white, with the snow blending the road, our windshields and the surrounding mountains together. It was a constant battle to try to wipe the snow off my windshield as I rode slowly along. It was impossible to see through it for most of the time, as it was high and designed to shield me from the wind. I was cold and wet, and after two hours of riding slowly through the snow, we stopped at a gas station to fuel up. I was happy that I had packed for this exact type of situation, and pulled out my spare pair of gloves and changed my socks to keep myself warm. Thankfully there was a small local restaurant right next to the gas station, so we all warmed ourselves with Turkish tea and indulged in a sweet honeycomb dessert. We chatted about where we would stop for the day, eventually deciding on the town of Amasya, which was about a two-hour ride from our current location. We figured we could endure the weather and the road conditions for that much longer before exhaustion might set upon us.

We hit the road again, our two wheeled beasts grinding up the kilometers quickly. It didn't seem as if any time had passed before we saw the welcome sign for Amasya, and we headed directly for the Hotel Sari Konak, which is located right along the river.

We had travelled an incredible 650 kilometers today, the longest distance so far since we had departed Canada. At home a journey of this length wouldn't take us more than maybe six hours, at maximum, but it had taken us more than ten hours today because of the weather conditions.

We were happy that our ride was over for the day, and we could have the evening to wind down.

We discovered that Amasya is another beautiful and historical town, which turns into heaven as the lights come on in the gathering darkness of the evening. The history here goes back an amazing 7500 years, and there is evidence of this throughout the town. The Ottoman era houses still exist here, as well as the tombs of former Pontus kings that were carved into the cliffs nearby. There is a lot to see here, including the former royal palace and the tombs of the kings of Pontus carved into the rock above the town, the Amasya Castle, along with many other delightful historic sites. Surprisingly, the town is also quite famous for their sweet apples.

I wanted to stretch my legs after the long drive, so after checking into the hotel and leaving my luggage, I joined Sukhvir Singh for a walk around the town. Just outside the hotel however, as we were making our way down the street, we were startled by someone calling out "Sardar Ji", which is a respectful term for someone wearing a turban. I turned quickly to see who might be addressing us in our native language, and discovered a gentleman walking towards us. He shook our hands and told us that he was amazed to see someone in Amasya wearing a turban. He was originally from Afghanistan and had been living in Amasya for several years and working at a local bakery, which produced Baklawa, one of the most popular treats in Turkey. We chatted for a moment before heading on our way, and I couldn't help thinking about how many interesting people we had met during our journey. How we, as people, touch each other's lives in so many small ways is astonishing. A simple hello or a smile can turn someone's day around, and a kind greeting in one's native language while travelling in a foreign country can impact one in a way that is inconceivable.

After a time of exploring the surrounding area, we returned to the hotel to meet up with the rest of the group for dinner. We wandered along the river looking for a place to eat and ended up in the Beyoglu Restaurant, for a fantastic meal of mouth-watering Turkish food and desserts. It had been a very long and challenging day, but as we made our way back to the hotel and our beds, we were smiling.

APRIL 22nd, 2019
MONDAY

We had decided that we wanted to bask in the beauty of the town and the warm friendliness of the locals for another day, so we enjoyed a leisurely breakfast in the hotel, savouring both the view of the river as well as the wonderful variety of Turkish cheeses that were included in the meal. It was going to be a good day to get a couple of things done, since we had some free time. The motorcycles needed to be serviced, so we had booked an appointment with MotoMax Honda. The group split up, with some of us going to the dealership to take care of the bikes, and myself and the others stayed behind to take care of reserving the hotel for one more night.

We had planned to only spend one night here, and it was a bit disappointing when I discovered that the hotel we were staying in was full and we needed to check out. With a bit of research, we decided to move to the Otel Tashan, which was close by. With the help of Jasmeet Singh and Mandeep Singh, we packed up everyone's belongings and transferred them to the new "otel" that we had booked for our additional night. We were learning a bit of the local language – otel means hotel in Turkish. We were happy to see that the new "otel" was more than acceptable, as it is a restored 17-century Ottoman inn with a spacious courtyard and wonderfully authentic guestrooms. The on-site restaurant even features Ottoman cuisine.

We were delighted to find, upon receipt of our bikes after servicing, that MotoMax Honda had not only given them the servicing that they required, but had also washed and polished them. It was like having brand new motorcycles all over again, as they looked as they had when we had rolled them out from Burnaby Kawasaki, six months ago. We were extremely satisfied with the performance of the KLR650's so far, and I was happy that we had made a good choice in our purchase of them.

Although we had only been taking care of the servicing and the change of hotel, we still felt as if we had been hustling all day, so we set out to explore the local market in the evening for some down time. It was almost a surreal experience, as the locals had not seen anyone before with turbans and beards. There were a few Turkish people who approached us, kissing our beards and turbans out of love and appreciation of who we were and what we looked like. They had never seen Sikh men before.

I was amused to see how many people wanted to take a photo with Jatinder Singh, because he sported the longest beard of all of us. The other person who was garnering a lot of attention was Jasmeet Singh, because he is a whopping six foot seven inches tall. His height was an oddity in most places we had travelled, as I hadn't yet seen anyone taller than him, but here the people were not afraid to approach him to ask for a picture.

I was blown away by the love, affection, genuine kindness and generosity of the local people in this town. We were invited into many shops and given souvenirs and the yummy Turkish tea that was now a staple in our day. These incredible people welcomed us, even though we didn't speak their language, and treated us like celebrities. This was one of the most memorable days so far, and this little historic town and its people will forever hold a special place in my heart.

We decided to return to the restaurant that we had enjoyed the night previous, as they had made us custom vegetarian dishes, before returning to the hotel to get some rest. It was sad to think that we couldn't spend any more time here, but the road beckoned and we had a mission to complete.

112 | Heading Home

APRIL 23rd, 2019
TUESDAY

After filling ourselves on what we considered to be a royal breakfast at the Hotel Tashan, we layered up our clothing to keep ourselves warm and dry during our ride today. We didn't know what type of weather we might encounter, and it was better to be safe than sorry.

Our bright yellow jackets and black riding pants always made us look impressive as a group. I felt that we were giving the right impression to those who observed us – that we were on a team on a mission. It was hard to think what people might imagine about our adventure as they saw us motoring down the highways.

While it had been a fantastic idea to have bright matching jackets to show people who we were, the idea of safety had also been a consideration. It is very important for motorcyclists to be seen, and having the yellow jackets was our way of, hopefully, allowing larger vehicles and drivers to see us more easily. It was almost as if our freshly washed and serviced motorcycles were itching to be on the road as much as we were, and it felt as if we were flying down the highway as we departed Amasya with our fond memories. We were headed to Erzincan, in northern Turkey, which was about a 375-kilometer ride through dense mountains. The hairpin turns were fun and exciting, but, needing more concentration for this type of riding, made it impossible for us to savour the passing scenery.

I was grateful for my warm clothing as we travelled through two snow-covered passes where the temperature was well below zero Celsius. It was a nice benefit that the highways were easy to follow and drivers respectfully understand that slower vehicles stay to the right. We knew that there were many speed cameras along the route, so we kept our eyes peeled for them, and constantly on our speedometers. The last thing any of us needed was a speeding ticket.

The changing scenery was stunning, as we came across volcanic domes that provided the landscape with a different color and shape. The land changed yet again as a flat and fertilized lowland appeared before us, surrounded by the high peaks of the mountains. That was our destination for the day.

The ancient town of Erzincan has been reformed into a modern, well organized city after sustaining major earthquakes in 1939 and again in 1992. Even with the modern buildings, the natural beauty surrounding the town had delighted us.

While we had managed to find our way through several other large cities and into small towns, for some reason we were having difficulty making our way to our hotel here. While standing at a roundabout and trying to figure out in which direction was the Hotel Eriza, a Turkish gentleman approached us and showed us his phone, where he had typed and translated the phrase, "May I help you?" His next translated message was, "I am a motorcyclist, too." When we told him where we were headed, he offered to let us follow him there. Our hotel happened to be just a short distance from the roundabout. When we reached the hotel and thanked him for his kind help, he explained again that he was a motorcyclist and invited us to join him for dinner.

We were a bit hesitant to head off for dinner with a complete stranger, so instead we declined, saying that we were tired from our more than six-hour ride. He continued to insist though, and we made an excuse that we needed to freshen up and then would join him, and went up to our rooms.

Sukhvir Singh, Jasmeet Singh and I eventually wandered our way back to the lobby and decided to take a walk together down the street to look at the shops. As we were walking, however, the same gentleman found us and asked us again to join him for dinner. We reluctantly agreed to pop into one of the restaurants around us, instead of travelling to a different area with him. It was awkward to continue to say no to him, as he was very polite about the situation, but it was hard to trust someone who had just come up to us out of the blue.

Just a few minutes after we had sat down at the table, two ladies and four other men arrived to join us. Our new friend had invited them, as they were all part of the same riding club. We snacked on Baklawa and Turkish tea while we commenced our chat about our machines and how long we had each been riding. They were amazed to hear about the adventure we were undertaking. They had never met a group of motorcyclists who had done something like this. It was an interesting encounter, as we got to know motorcyclists from another country who shared nothing but the same passion for riding as we did. I was feeling bad that we had avoided having a proper dinner with him, but in the end, I think we all enjoyed ourselves.

We said goodbye to our new acquaintances and walked the short distance back towards the hotel, intending to meet up with the rest of the group to have a full dinner, but I was sidetracked by the possibility of shopping for some leather boots, as I had heard that the leather goods in Turkey were of very good quality. I was pleased to find some that were reasonably priced and returned to the hotel with my purchase. We met up with the rest of the group to try one of the nearby restaurants for our evening meal. With our stomachs full of great food, we talked about the next phase of the trip, which would be another adventure. We had to walk off the meal before bed, so we strolled along and were rewarded with a view of the lights of the town in the evening darkness, giving us the feeling as if we were wandering our way into a painting.

It was time for the day to end, and we headed to our rooms to warm up and snuggle into the comfortable beds for a good night's sleep.

APRIL 24th, 2019
WEDNESDAY

Our ultimate destination today was the city of Erzurum, which was about 275 kilometers from Erzincan, but an early departure was in order, as we wanted to avoid any potential bad weather and had no desire to ride in the dark. It was nice to be able to beat the morning rush hour traffic. While we had an idea of which hotel we might stay in tonight, there was also the concern that rooms might not be available and we would need extra time to look for another appropriate hotel.

As we were getting ready to leave, I received a message from our new acquaintance of the evening before, asking if we would join him for breakfast before leaving town. I was sad to reply that we were leaving soon and regretfully would not be able to. We grabbed a quick breakfast right at the hotel, settled our belongings in their places, and mounted our steeds once again.

We were making our way out of Erzincan and towards the route that would lead us to Erzurum, when we were forced to pull over to the side of the road by an unmarked van. Concerned that something was happening that would affect our safety, we all pulled over into a petrol-station and looked for a place to park, wondering what it was all about. Before we had even settled our motorcycles on their pedestals, another vehicle joined the first one, making me very suspicious of their intentions.

As they approached us, we were informed that they were undercover police, and that they had received a complaint about us filming while we were riding. We explained who we were and what we were doing, and the situation quickly defused, although the interrogation and investigation lasted well over an hour. The police were strict in their instructions to not film anything while we were riding, but in the end, they wished us luck and apologized for bothering us. It was after eleven in the morning when we were finally allowed to pull back out onto the highway and continue our journey.

It had been a bit of a strange encounter that had shaken us a bit, and I tried to put it out of my mind as we motored forward. I pondered several other things as I rode, trying to get the incident out of my head, one being that I had recognized a Turkish word "hava" on a sign nearby where we had been parked, which meant air in Turkish, and wondered at the mysteries of language, as "hava" also means air in Punjabi.

My random thoughts were soon replaced by the concentration it took to ride through the mountains, and my eyes darted here and there, trying to soak in everything at once. The road passed along some higher altitudes and the snow at the higher levels constantly reminded me of being in Canada. It had been three weeks since we left Vancouver, and I had to admit, even though I was enjoying the trip, I was feeling a bit homesick.

The city of Erzurum appeared before us along the long and open road that stretches across the eastern half of the country. It has some of the finest winter sports facilities in Turkey, and even though that was not the reason for us being there, we decided to book ourselves into a resort high on the mountain that was world famous for its skiing – the Hotel Polat. It was luxurious to indulge in their relaxation activities, as we soaked in the pool and treated ourselves to a Turkish steam room treatment.

Relaxed and refreshed, we wanted to explore the city, as it is a modern, metropolitan city with huge shopping complexes. Being the shopping addict that I am, I was itching to buy some more leather goods and check out the fine cotton items that I knew were for sale. Turkey is well known for its leather and cotton goods, and it seemed like a fine idea to spend some of our down time wandering the shopping areas.

I was pleased to find a unique pair of leather shoes in blue and camel coloring, along with a beautiful cotton floral shirt and grey pants. The others in the group

also found some great items, from leather boots to jackets. We were once again set upon by the locals asking for pictures with us, which we gladly obliged.

The city has other delightful things to see as well, including the most photogenic site, which is the Cifte Minareli Medrese, which is a twin columned school that dates back to the 13th century. The sparsely spaced blue tiles pop out wonderfully, complimenting the red brickwork of each minaret. There are other interesting historic sites within the city, as the length of human occupation of this area dates back to 4,000 B.C., so along with the excellent skiing to be had here, it's worth a visit to this gem.

We relished in the view that was provided to us at the hotel, as the resort was located high on the mountain, and our rooms were on the seventh floor. We returned to the hotel before the night was too late, and appreciated the pretty view of the city lights before heading to bed early.

APRIL 25th, 2019
THURSDAY

It was to be another short riding day, of only 275 kilometers, so we weren't in a hurry to eat breakfast or leave the hotel. I had slept well and woke feeling happy and bright, but as the morning passed, I found a sense of uneasiness descend over me. The breakfast area of the hotel had been almost completely taken over by men in military uniforms, making us wonder what was happening in the area that so many were billeted there.

The evening prior when we arrived, I had noticed that there had been a couple of uniformed men replacing a license plate on a nearby Volvo, covering up the one that was already there. It had occurred to me to say something to someone about the activity, but I realized that there was no one to speak to about it so I had put it out of my mind. Now, I recalled the strange actions of the men and wondered if that was related to what was happening this morning.

We looked for an empty table to claim and sat down quietly, feeling very awkward. We weren't sure if this was normal or not. As we rose again to help ourselves to the buffet, then returned to the table to fill our empty bellies, we whispered amongst ourselves, trying to make light of the tense atmosphere. What would happen if one of us dropped a fork? Would they all stand up and pull their guns out? We weren't sure. We finished our breakfast in silence, uncomfortable in the quietness of the room. It was a relief to return to our rooms to gather our belongings and don our riding gear.

It didn't take us long to finish preparing to head out, and soon our wheels were spinning down the highway towards the last town in Turkey before crossing over into Iran. The drive continued to take us through the now familiar mountains, and I couldn't get enough of the beautiful scenery as we rode.

Dogubayazit stands on a flat plain, shadowed by Turkey's highest peak, Mount Ararat. This mountain is considered one of the holiest sites for Armenians, and is supposedly where Noah's Ark landed. With a qualified local guide and the right permits, if you have the time, you can climb this mountain. The Ishak Pasa Palace, which lies on a hill 5 kilometers to the south outside the city, is an ancient fortress, castle and mosque which is stunningly beautiful. There are a couple of other interesting sites in the area, which unfortunately we did not have time to visit.

The climate of the plain was cold and dry and we were definitely feeling the effects of the weather as we headed straight to our hotel, which was the Hotel Golden Hill. Leaving our bikes right outside the main entrance to the hotel, we checked in, dropped our luggage in our rooms and stripped off our heavy riding gear, before heading out to dinner.

Without knowing the language, it was difficult to converse with the taxi driver, and yet he still managed to take us to the best restaurant in town. The manager at the Ararat Restaurant made us the best vegetarian soup, pizza and dessert, and we left feeling full and satisfied. We discovered a carpet store right next to the restaurant and went in to check out the fine quality carpets on display. There was everything from classic to modern style carpets, ranging all the way up to $300,000 USD. While I appreciated the beauty of the carpets for sale, my limited cargo space on the bike would make it impossible to take one home with me.

We returned to the hotel at a decent hour, as we wanted to get a good night's sleep. Our plan was to be at the border by seven in the morning, so we required an early rise. I was excited to be entering Iran, but several worrying thoughts were still running through my head. There were restrictions about usage of Facebook, and we wouldn't be able to connect with the outside world and our well-wishers through that social media method until we left the country. I wasn't sure what to expect with the border crossing or travel through Iran, but I calmed myself as I fell asleep by the thought that it was just another part of the adventure and whatever was meant to happen would happen.

APRIL 26th, 2019
FRIDAY

The alarm on my cell phone beeped its morning song to wake me, and I shut it off quickly before it also woke my roommate – Jasmeet Singh – who had been sharing rooms with me since the beginning of the trip. I finished my morning routine as quickly as possible so that he could have his turn in the bathroom to get ready for the day. The rest of the team was already waiting for us when we descended to the hotel restaurant for breakfast. The service from the staff was fantastic, as we had told them that we would be departing early, and they had ensured that our breakfast would be ready for us. It didn't take us long for the morning meal though, as we were all anxious to be on our way. In our rooms once again, we donned the heavy riding gear, grabbed our personal belongings and departed.

The unknown elements of entering Iran weighed on us along with the excitement of crossing the border, and I prayed we would have an easy time entering the country. We had heard a lot of things about the country and we wanted to have the best experience possible. The Iranian visa had been the most difficult one to get and because of this, and the little knowledge that we had about travelling through the country, uneasiness was evident amongst our group members.

Dogubayazit is located a short 30 kilometers away from the Iranian border, and it didn't take us long to reach it as the traffic was light at this time of the morning. The journey only took us a half an hour, but we had forgotten there was a time difference, so we arrived later than we had planned.

Along the route we spied some men in uniform with assault weapons jogging behind an armoured vehicle. The vehicle had the rear door open and a ladder hanging from it. I was puzzled by the sight, and using the handsfree communications set that we had, asked the rest of the group the questions that were on my mind. If these trained men with guns required an armoured vehicle for patrolling, was the ladder there so that they could quickly get inside if they were ambushed or someone started shooting at them? And if so, what would happen to a motorcyclist who happened to get caught in the crossfire? Everyone laughed when I answered my own question, stating that if we were smart enough, we wouldn't be doing what we were doing.

We arrived at the Iranian border to meet our guide. It was a requirement to have a guide with us at all times when in the country, and we had made arrangements with the Iran Traveling Center, where I had dealt with a lovely lady by the name of Mahtab Emami, who had been most helpful with everything.

She had provided us with a local guide named Hesam Yousefi, who was waiting for us at the border and helped us with all the paperwork. By the time we finished the basics, it was already afternoon.

Upon meeting Hesam, he provided us with some devastating news – we would not be able to ride our motorcycles through the country. We were absolutely heartbroken by the news. The border officials had informed Hesam that because our bikes were 650cc, the engine size was too big. Neither us, nor Hesam, knew of this new law which had just come into effect in the country. We tried to convince the officials ourselves, with no luck. We had to start to look for an alternative way of not only us crossing the country, but our bikes as well. After a long discussion, Hesam recommended that we ship the bikes using a truck that could take them all the way to the border of Pakistan. None of us were pleased with the solution, but we couldn't see any way around it. Reluctantly we agreed.

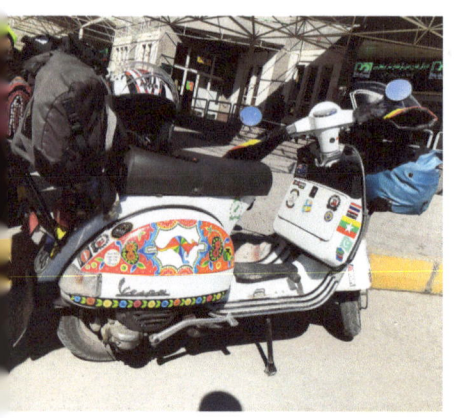

During our wait, we met a lovely couple from Australia who were travelling on a Vespa Scooter. They were crossing into Turkey, and we got to chatting. They had already been on the road for forty-five days, much longer than we had. Of course, we had to take a photo with them, and added our Sikh Motorcycle Club sticker to the many they already had on their scooter. It was a pleasure to meet them and a nice diversion from our troubles.

The day was waning and Hesam was still dealing with everything, so he advised us to travel by taxi into the border town of Bazargan. We were tired and hungry, so this idea appealed to us, and we hopped into the cabs that Hesam arranged for us to head to the Hotel Shahryar Bazargan. The hotel's restaurant was informed that we were all vegetarians and provided us with appropriate meals.

I was impressed, because as we were having our meal, Hesam continued to make phone calls to find a reliable trucking company to transport our bikes. I had been in contact with him prior to the trip and had found him very nice and professional, and he was proving that he could take care of things for us. I was grateful that we had him along with us. After eating, we wearily trekked to our rooms for a bit of rest, and to absorb what had happened. It was incredibly disappointing and I had to keep reminding myself that everything happens for good, and that I needed to stay positive. It was hard to relax while we still didn't know what tomorrow would bring, but Hesam eventually found a company that he was satisfied with and informed us that the truck had been booked and would be waiting to load in the morning.

Later, we enjoyed a falafel sandwich for dinner and were absolutely amazed at the variety of local bread and naans that were available at every store. The day hadn't gone as planned, but we were safe and taken care of, so all was well.

APRIL 27th, 2019
SATURDAY

My alarm was set for seven in the morning, and we were down in the lobby by eight o'clock to find that Hesam was already there waiting for us. He was busy on a phone call, which sounded like he was checking when the truck might arrive. As he finished his call, he confirmed what I had thought. The truck would soon be at the trucking yard, next to the holding area where we had left the bikes.

This morning we walked back to where the motorcycles were stored, and were allowed to ride them the short distance to where the truck was waiting to load them. I was happy to see that the truck was ready and waiting for us, but surprised that there was no proper loading dock to get the bikes onto the truck. With all my experience with trucking, I wanted to make sure that our precious bikes would be stored and tied down correctly. If not, there was a chance that they would be damaged or scratched.

We used a ramp to get the bikes up into the truck, one by one. The Iranian truck driver seemed very professional, but I was still concerned. This was a big deal, letting the bikes go without us. We double and triple checked that the bikes were stowed and tied properly, then ensured that the truck was sealed. I also made sure that there was a GPS tracking device with the sealed door. To be safe, I took photos of the truck, the GPS device, the license plates and the driver. At least we would have some proof of who had our bikes if something were to happen.

The new scenario had made us make major changes in our travelling plans. Instead of riding, we would have to travel by car and by plane to get to where we wanted to go. By the time the motorcycles were loaded and the truck ready to roll off, Hesam had booked us a flight from Tabrez to Tehran, which was to depart at 18:25. Tabrez was about 275 kilometers from where we were, so he took the liberty and hired two taxis to take us to the airport without wasting any more time. It was about a three-and-a-half-hour drive, so we needed to get going, as it was already almost noon when we finished loading.

Along the route to Tabrez we were pulled over a couple of times by roadblocks and teams of armed men. Thankfully, Hesam did the talking and none of the rest of us were questioned or asked to get out of the vehicles. This was an entirely new experience for us and I was seeing why it was so necessary to have a local guide travel along with us. We reached the Tabrez airport with enough time to catch our flight. I wasn't surprised to see that we were the only people in the airport, or on the flight, wearing turbans.

The flight was a short hour and fifteen minutes, but by the time we landed and disembarked, we didn't leave the Tehran airport until about eight thirty in the evening. We went straight to the Hotel Espinas International, where we were booked in to stay the night. It is located in downtown Tehran, about 60 kilometers from the airport, which took us more than an hour and a half to drive in the evening traffic.

Tehran is the capital of Iran, with an incredible city population of about nine million, not including the outlying areas. It has been the capital of the country, on and off, since 1786, which means there is some history here, even though a good majority of the city was rebuilt in the early 1900's. The people here speak Persian, and the majority of Tehranis are officially Twelver Shia Muslims, which has also been the state religion since the 16th-century Safavid conversion. Being one of the main tourism destinations in the country, the city has a wealth of cultural and historical attractions, along with many shopping opportunities.

We had chosen to book into the Hotel Espinas, which is one of the best hotels in Tehran, and we found a lot of other foreigners staying there. Hesam was in possession of all of our passports, as is the protocol, and handed them over to the hotel when we arrived. We had planned to spend one night here originally, but because of the change of circumstances, we would be extending our stay to two nights.

We sat down for dinner in the hotel restaurant and discussed our upcoming days activities with Hesam, along with the new plan for the days leading up to our pickup of the bikes at the border of Pakistan. Hesam was very polite, well educated and knew what he was doing. I felt good that we were in his capable hands. He conveyed our plan with Mahtab Emami at the Iran Traveling Center, so that they would know what was happening, and we ended the day with a promise to meet for breakfast at eight o'clock the next morning.
We split up as we went to our rooms for the evening. It had been an exhausting day, dealing with the unexpected things that had been thrown at us, but we had to let the chips fall as they may, and try to enjoy as much as we could.

"ALL THINGS WORK TOGETHER FOR GOOD."

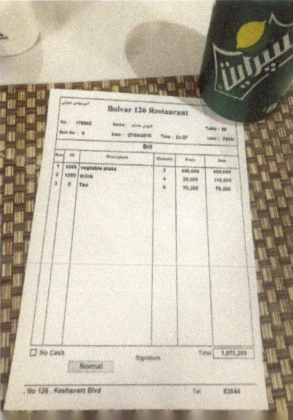

APRIL 28th, 2019
SUNDAY

We met at our coordinated time in the Hotel Espinas's restaurant to have breakfast before we went out adventuring for the day. I was delighted to see that there was a lot of fresh food being prepared and served, which was a new experience for us for breakfast. There were lots of different types of dates available at the buffet bar, and we sampled as many as we could. Everything was delicious and a wonderful way to begin the day.

As we devoured our meal, I took the opportunity to observe the others in the restaurant. Iran has some strict laws about dress and behaviour, among other things, and one of these laws is that all ladies must cover their heads. I was accustomed to seeing Sikh women having their heads covered, but the law here meant that even female tourists need to wear a head covering, and this was a strange sight for me. I reminded myself, there were laws that affected men as well when it came to dress codes. Even though Iran can, at times, be very hot, men are not allowed to wear shorts.

It wasn't long before we finished satisfying our hunger and returned to our rooms to get ourselves ready for the day out in the city. I decided to go with bright colors and dressed in a floral shirt I had bought in Turkey and a mustard-coloured turban. It didn't matter if the colours would make me stand out, as I knew that no matter where we went, we were going to receive attention from the general public.

Hesam had hired a van that would accommodate all of us for the day, to take us wherever we would like to go. By the time we had finished making ourselves presentable, both Hesam and the driver were waiting for us in the lobby.

We decided to start our day with a prayer session and to seek blessings by visiting Gurdwara Bhai Ganga Singh Sabha, the only Gurdwara Sahib in Tehran. I had spoken to Sahib Singh, the administrator of Gurdwara Sahib, when I started planning this trip eighteen months ago, so it was a wonderful feeling to finally be visiting. We arrived to find that only ten people were present, even though it was Sunday, and I remembered that Sunday is considered a weekday in Iran.

Before entering the main hall, we stopped to take off our shoes and store them in the appropriate area, where Guru Granth Sahib was displayed. We were approached by an Iranian Sikh who asked us who the person accompanying us was. When we explained that it was our local guide, he told us that Hesam was not allowed in the main hall. This was a shock to us, as Gurdwaras around the world welcome all, no matter who they are, as long as their heads are covered, they are dressed appropriately, and have taken off their shoes.

The explanation continued as we questioned the administrators, who told us that the Iranian government had asked them not to allow people of other faiths to enter the main hall. It was a horrible feeling to tell Hesam that he couldn't join us, but he accepted gracefully, being familiar with the legal restriction.

It was exciting to be able to spend some time with Sahib Singh, who gave us some information about Gurdwara Sahib and the Punjabi school which was part of it. The school teaches Punjabi along with the syllabus required by the Iranian government. We were served some tea and snacks, then said our goodbyes, promising to return for evening prayers.

Our next stop was at the Grand Bazaar, which is one of the oldest and biggest bazaars in the world. The floods of people along the narrow streets amazed me, and we were almost overwhelmed by the sheer number of people crowded throughout the Bazaar. We took a moment to stop for fresh juice before diving in. As usual, we were drawing attention to ourselves just by being us, with our full beards and turbans. There are some Iranians who wear turbans, but most of them are Mulas (religious leaders) or government officials. The locals could easily recognize that we were neither of those.

From the Bazaar, we headed to Golestan Palace (Gulistan Palace), which is also sometimes known as the Rose Garden Palace. The glamourous history of Iran is fully on display here as it is a spectacular example of Persian art, history, and architecture. The palace was established during Safavid era (1501 – 1736) and the next dynasties added to this structure, so today the complex consists of seventeen palaces, museums, and halls.

Of course, we couldn't miss seeing the Daria-i-Noor diamond at the Iranian National Jewels Museum, so that was next on our list of things to do. Daria-i-Noor means "sea of light" in Persian, and this magnificent gem is one of the largest cut diamonds in the world, weighing an estimated 182 carats. Its colour, pale pink, is one of the rarest to be found in diamonds. Understandably, the museum had lots of security and we were made to go through lots of scanning before being allowed to enter.

There was so much to see in the city that we were having a hard time getting everything in, but there was one more place that was a must see for us, and that was the statue of Abul-Qâsem Ferdowsi Tusi, also known as Firdawsi. Sometimes referred to as Ferdowsi, he was a Persian poet and the author of Shahnameh, which is one of the world's longest epic poems created by a single poet. Ferdowsi's name is mentioned in the Zafarnama, the letter of victory, written by Guru Gobind Singh, the 10th Master of Sikhs.

We returned to Gurdwara Bhai Ganga Singh Sabha in time for evening prayer and discovered a lot more people present than had been there in the morning. We encountered numerous ladies who were anxiously waiting to welcome us and talk about the purpose of our travels. They expressed how proud they were to be part of the same faith and community that would promote such a mission. We were amazed, as always, as our new acquaintances claimed that they would love to be doing what we were doing.

The more people that told us this, the more I surprised I was. I hadn't thought that this would be something that many people would be interested in doing. We were happy to receive a donation from the Gurdwara administration during the evening, and the gratitude I felt towards everyone that had welcomed us was an incredible feeling.

We were blessed to be invited to share a meal at Gurdwara Sahib which had been specially prepared for us, and we passed the time pleasantly speaking to all who had gathered. The hours flew by and before we knew it, the time had come to return to the hotel.

On our return journey, Hesam told us how very much moved he was by the way local Sikhs were treating us. Before bed, we sat for awhile in the lobby of the hotel to talk about what would happen the next day. Satisfied with our plan, we all headed to our respective rooms for a good night's sleep.

APRIL 29th, 2019
MONDAY

Despite wanting to wake early to partake of the same excellent breakfast I had enjoyed the morning previous, I slept in a bit, but thankfully still managed to make it downstairs in time to fill my stomach with freshly made goodies and fruit. Hesam was cheerfully waiting in the restaurant, and learning that he had already eaten, I was concerned about my tardiness, but was reassured that I could take my time. Hesam left us to enjoy the meal and asked us to meet him in the lobby when we were finished. I was intrigued, as it sounded as if he had a change of plan that he wanted to discuss with us.

During a conversation the evening before, Hesam had asked us if we would like to go with him to visit his village and see where he was building a facility for hikers and horseback riding. It was a lovely invitation and we couldn't refuse. Throughout the past days I had been very grateful for his friendliness and cheerful, helpful attitude. He worked so well with the constantly changing plans that I knew that he had been put with us for a reason.

Upon completing our meal, we met him in the lobby, where he told us that he had been thinking that we should plan to stay another day in Tehran, as there was nothing much to explore or do in Zahedan, which was our next destination. It was a good suggestion and we all agreed to it readily.

With a promise to return to the lobby in a half an hour, we all spent some time in our rooms preparing for the day. When we found ourselves in the lobby again, the transport and Hesam were waiting patiently for us. It only took us a minute to get situated in the comfortable van and be on the road towards Aghchari, the village where Hesam lived. It was exciting to think that we were going to experience a bit of Iranian life outside the city.

It was interesting to travel the 150 kilometers to the village, which took us a couple of hours to drive. It was nice to be able to stare out the window at the passing scenery without having to worry about watching the road or driving in a strange country. We arrived in the tiny village to find that it had a population of just over one hundred people, but the area is still well known for the special horse breeding center nearby.

We made a quick stop at the local grocery store and ran into Hesam's father while there, which was a pleasure. With the journey complete, we stopped at Hesam's place and were treated to some fresh watermelon before we walked over to the stables, which were located about a kilometer from his house. Hesam offered the opportunity to ride one of the horses, which a couple of our group members took advantage of, but I was not brave enough to. Being on an iron horse is one thing, being on a four-legged horse with a mind of its own is something else completely. The day had passed quickly and, after checking our watches, we decided that it was time to return to the city, to attend a dinner to which we had been invited to by Mrs. Renu Sethi, who we had met at the Gurdwara Sahib the previous day. We got caught up in the late afternoon traffic, which caused us to spend about three hours navigating the route, arriving at about seven in the evening.

They had prepared a special Iranian meal for us, with all the wonderful flavours of the real food of the country. Typically, Iranian main dishes are combinations of rice with meat, vegetables, and nuts, but obviously, since we were vegetarians, no meat was included. Characteristic Iranian flavorings such as saffron, dried lime and other sources of sour flavoring, cinnamon, turmeric, and parsley are mixed and used in various dishes, and herbs are frequently used, along with fruits such as plums, pomegranates, quince, prunes, apricots, and raisins.

It was thoughtful of them to have prepared not just the Iranian meal, but also some chapatis, just in case one of us didn't like the meal that was presented to us. We were honoured, because Mrs. Sethi explained that they only cooked chapatis for special occasions. The cook was a local Iranian woman, and her food was utterly fantastic. We spent the evening discussing the situation of Sikhs in Iran, along with many other subjects. Mr. and Mrs. Sethi explained that in the past, Sikhs had a bigger community within Iran, but a lot of the younger generations were leaving in favour of living in western countries. With only the older generations left in Iran, it looked like there was a significant decline of numbers in the Sikh community. Being an older couple, they had spent their whole lives in Iran, and they were looking forward to remaining there for the rest of their days. They couldn't necessarily understand why the younger people wanted to leave so badly and I was wondering the same thing. Even though I had emigrated to Canada in my younger years, I pondered what would have to change in the country to ensure that the younger generation would stay and make their lives there. It was an excellent question, but I had no answers and instead contented myself with listening to their commentary. The night was getting on, and our beds were calling for us, so we thanked the Sethi family for their hospitality and set out for the hotel. It had been a tiring, but wonderful day, and I silently thanked everyone we had spent time with as we arrived to our rooms. The unexpected experiences were making this change of itinerary very gratifying.

It was almost midnight when I finally fell into bed. I thought I would fall asleep instantly, but I just couldn't shut my mind off. I was pondering the current situation of the younger generations of Sikhs in Iran and thinking about the lives that we were blessed with in Canada. As I drifted off into sleep, I thanked God for allowing us to have a life where whole families could live together, just as we did in Punjab. I recognized, as my eyes closed with tiredness, that Canada is not only a land of opportunities for immigrants, but also for their Canadian born children and grandchildren, and all the generations that would follow.

APRIL 30th, 2019
TUESDAY

It had been a enjoyable couple of days in Tehran and the area, but today we needed to get back into travelling and we were scheduled to leave for Zahedan on a flight in the afternoon. We didn't need to be at the airport until about one o'clock in the afternoon though, so this meant that we could relax a bit in the morning and take our time getting ready.

I relished the idea of once again having the delicious breakfast that I had become accustomed to over the past few mornings. A leisurely meal was followed by some time repacking up our bags and checking out, along with some last-minute photos of the hotel, our group and the area. It was almost eleven thirty by the time, Sukhvir Singh and I finished up our photo shoot and loaded the van with our possessions and the rest of the group members.

I had asked Hesam to let us make one more stop before going to the airport, so that we could see the Azadi Gate, which is a famous landmark in Iran. As a silent witness to Iran's major historical events, this tower remains Tehran's most iconic landmark. Standing guard like a sentry at the gates of Tehran, the "Freedom Tower" was built in 1971 and comprised of eight thousand white marble blocks. A combination of both Islamic and Sassanid architectural styles, the fifty-foot-high tower commemorates the formation of the Persian Empire and is an interesting combination of both modern and ancient cultures. We tumbled out of the van and soon all six of us were posing with this unique monument, trying to make sure we could capture the whole thing in the frame behind us. Azadi (Freedom) means a lot to every human being and this monument spoke to all of us.

We didn't want to have to rush to get our flight, so as soon as we were finished enjoying the tower, we jumped back in the van to finish the drive to the airport. It was difficult to say goodbye to our driver, as he was a very kind, soft-spoken, professional man who had been with us for the past few days. We commemorated the time with him with a photo and said our goodbyes.

It didn't take us long to get checked in for the flight and head to the boarding gate, but it seemed as if we had only been relaxing for a moment before the flight was called and boarding commenced. The two-hour flight passed quickly as we spent the time planning the next phase of our adventure.

It was only mid-afternoon when we landed at the Zahedan airport. The green pastures of the country had changed to brown, barren landscapes that were still impressive in their own way. It almost seemed as if we had entered another country, as the scenery was so different from where we had been.

Before the rise of Reza Shah Pahlavi in 1923, the city of Zahedan was known as Dozz-aab, literally meaning "water thief". This is the name given to a sandy land formation that quickly swallows up any water that falls on it, be it rain or irrigation water. The name was changed to Zahedan ("Sages," or "pious people" in Persian) during the reign of Reza Shah Pahlavi in the 1930s. It is believed that when Reza Shah visited the city, he saw Sikhs in white robes living there and thus changed the name to Zahedan after them, who were considered Zahid (pious) by him. Turbaned people are still very much respected here.

Our first destination was the Esteghlal Grand Hotel, where we checked in and left our luggage before going to Gurdwara Singh Sabha, which was the first gurdwara outside of India. Hesam was so touched by everything that was going on that he insisted that I tie a turban around his head before arriving to Gurdwara. This gurdwara is almost one hundred years old, but unfortunately only serves less than ten Sikh families who still live in the area.

It was a distinct pleasure to meet Shami Singh, whom I had spoken to a year previous, while planning the ride. To me, meeting these people and seeing these places was like living a dream. All the places that I had thought about while planning, and the people I had talked to so long ago were all reality now.

We learned a little about the area and the history of Sikhs in the town from Shami Singh, as he explained that the government offices here still addressed Sikhs with much respect and provided them priority services. The local cab drivers were also known to not charge Sikhs for rides.

We also were told about the Punjabi School, which was at the Gurdwara Sahib, and had been there from the 1930's to 1952, before it was moved to Tehran. Shami Singh proudly explained that there were registers for student's attendance to the school dating back to 1935. The sad part of his explanation was that there were less than ten Sikh families living in Zahedan, mostly older residents whose children had left for India or other countries to study and live.

It was also interesting to get to know about Sant Baba Harnam Singh Ji, for his enlightenment teachings of the Sikh religion, through meditation of "Naam-Simran." We attended the evening ceremony and were presented with Langar, which had been prepared by the families in the Gurdwara.

The hardworking nature of the people of this town was evident in an older gentleman who had situated himself outside the Gurdwara building, sharing the message of 'Kirat Karo' (earning a living). He was selling samosas and believed in earning his living by working, no matter how old he was. A local informed us that this man was well known for his delicious samosas all over town. Listening to this man speak and seeing him living such an example of honest living touched me and I couldn't stop myself from shedding a few tears. I thanked God for giving me such a beautiful life and strong faith.

The memory of that evening would live forever in our hearts.

We planned to depart early the following morning for Mirjaveh, the border town which was located about 80 kilometers from where we were. It would be about an hour drive, and we were all excited to be reunited with our motorcycles and be able to get back on the road.

I am not sure how long it took me to go to sleep as I lay thinking about the rest of our upcoming journey and a strange mixture of excitement and sadness came over me. This was our last night in Iran, and I was anxious to enter Pakistan the following morning, the country where my parents and grandparents had been born.

MAY 1st, 2019
WEDNESDAY

It was an early start for us this morning, but since we were anxious to get on our way, it wasn't difficult to rise in time to have breakfast before departing. In fact, it seemed as if we were right on schedule, as by the time we were in the dining area of the hotel partaking of our meal, there were a few uniformed, armed men waiting to escort us to the border. Hesam explained that they were Iranian military personnel and they were going to take us to the Pakistan border at Taftan. He reassured us that there was nothing to worry about, it was part of the normal protocol for security in this region. It was a bit daunting to think that we needed to have a security escort, but I knew that this was only the beginning of our time with armed men. There was more yet to come. I had tried to prepare myself and the others for this, but being in the moment of it happening was something else entirely.

The only thoughts in our minds were how much we wanted to get back on our iron horses and ride. Our ultimate destination of Amritsar, Punjab, was finally within reach. Hesam informed us that the truck with our bikes was already waiting for us in Mirjaveh and we could unload ourselves when we arrived.

It didn't take us long to finish breakfast, gather our personal items and head out. We were separated into two vehicles, which were positioned behind a police car as we left. Two officers were accompanying us, and two others were driving behind us, armed with AK-47's. It was a true motorcade, and Jatinder Singh and I couldn't help giggling a bit as we drove away – even with the seriousness of the situation we were feeling a bit like royalty.

It took almost two hours to arrive to Mirjaveh, even though it was only a distance of about 80 kilometers, as there were numerous security checks along the route. The truck driver was patiently waiting for us, and I was overjoyed to see him. We were within walking distance of the border and we were all impatient to get out of our vehicles and get the motorcycles off the truck. It was time to enter Pakistan.

Heading Home | 149

We inspected each bike as we rolled them off the truck and found them to be in perfect shape. With a bit of time spent pulling on our riding gear and situating our saddle bags and items, we were ready to roll in a relatively short period of time. The Iranian border officials stamped out our Carnets for the bikes and the moment had come to depart Iran and enter Pakistan.

It was not easy to say goodbye to Hesam, as he had become a friend in the days that we had spent together. He had generously donated to Khalsa Aid in support of us and we made sure we took a last group photo with him before we happily swung our legs over our machines and revved up to ride away.

The morning had passed quickly and it was already one o'clock in the afternoon by the time we were ready to enter the country of Pakistan. We were going to be officially starting our time in the country in the Baluchistan province, which is considered the wild west of Pakistan. It was incredible to me that the first word I heard when entering the country was 'Sardar Ji'. This is a respectful term to speak to someone who wears a turban, and sometimes can mean the head or the leader. Hearing this, my heart sung and I felt a surge of happiness wash over me. It is amazing how one phrase can bring so much emotion.

We entered the immigration facility and were greeted by a long lineup of people waiting. We took our place in line and prepared ourselves for a long wait, but soon after we arrived, we were approached by a Border Security officer who brought us forward to complete our paperwork as priority travellers. We were a little confused at the situation, and mentioned to the officer that the other people had been waiting before us, most of whom were Pakistani nationals who were trying to return to their country after visiting holy shrines in Iran. The officer's response surprised us - "Tusi sade mehmaan ho" – which means "you are our guests". While we all felt proud of being Sikhs, I looked at the long lineup of people waiting and felt a little guilty that they were not treated the same way.

The Customs Officer offered us some juice while we were completing the paperwork, giving us the feeling of warm welcome to Pakistan. Everyone was pleasant and helpful, and the time seemed to pass quickly, even though it was close to three in the afternoon when they were finished with our passports and Carnets. Finishing up with the immigration officials, we were asked to follow one of the Levies vehicles to a gated facility in Taftan, just a few hundred meters from the border. The Balochistan Levies is a paramilitary gendarmerie, and operates as one of two primary law enforcement agencies tasked with maintaining law and order in the province.

The Levies station that we were taken to was a run-down concrete compound, consisting of jail cells and equally decrepit common rooms. Once inside the courtyard, we were told that this would be our home for the night. We looked around in dismay, this wasn't what we had been expecting. Every guard was equipped with an AK-47, which is considered the best gun there is. Thankfully, it was easy for us to communicate with the guards, as we were able to understand Urdu, and speak Hindi to them. The languages are very similar and I was grateful that we would be able to ask for something if required. It was interesting to experience the special treatment that we were receiving because of being Sikhs and being Canadian citizens.

It was now late in the day and we were all starving. We hadn't eaten anything since breakfast, but as I looked around, I couldn't see anywhere to get anything to eat. We finally asked one of the guards if we were allowed to go out to get a meal, and he responded, giving us the option of being accompanied to purchase food to bring back to the compound.

Sukhvir Singh and I coordinated with the guards, and soon after we were accompanied to a local restaurant a short distance away. We purchased some cooked okra, red kidney beans and a lot of naans, along with plenty of cold drinks. We wanted to ensure that if we were hungry later on, we would have enough. The two guards stood beside us as we ordered and waited for our food.

Returning to the rest of the group, we all tucked in quickly, relieving our rumbling stomachs. As we were eating, some young Pakistani boys came up to us for a chat. They told us that they were from the Punjab state of Pakistan and had been arrested and brought here by the Levies. With a bit of digging into their story, we discovered that they had been arrested by the Iranian police while trying to enter Iran illegally, and had been handed over to the Pakistani officials. They hadn't eaten for two days. It was a blessing that we had purchased so much, as we were able to share the rest of our meal with them. I silently sent up a thank you to God for being able to provide the boys with some much-needed nourishment.

As the sweltering night grew late, we tried to settle into what we needed to consider our "home sweet home" for the evening, but it was proving difficult. We were in an unused office with no ventilation, just one lonely fan turning its blades in the hot air, not providing any relief whatsoever. I was thankful that we had better accommodations that those occupying the jail cells on the other side of the courtyard, as they were all filled with garbage and smelled faintly of urine. As I tried to relax, I told myself that we would be fine – it was only one night.

We were all keeping in mind that we would be leaving early the next morning with an armed escort, and that our entire journey through the province would be dependent on them, so we needed to get some rest and have patience with any situation that presented itself. To ensure safety, an armed escort is provided to foreigners throughout the more than 700-kilometer journey through the province of Baluchistan. The next few days we would be at the mercy of the Levies and their schedule.

MAY 2nd, 2019
THURSDAY

I had done a lot of research and had read a lot about travel through this area while planning our motorcycle ride, but even with that knowledge, I still wasn't sure what today, or the following days, were going to look like. This was not the type of travel or riding that we had been doing for the past four weeks and we all needed to start this part of the journey with open minds.

We rose early and washed with the available bucket full of water to get the sticky grit off of us. It was no refreshing cold shower but better than nothing. We all tied Dumala (warrior style turban) on, as they are ideal for riding. We donned our regular motorcycle gear and our yellow jackets, still feeling pleased with the fact that we looked like a professional team of motorcycle riders. These little details made us feel united even in challenging circumstances.

Our escort vehicle arrived at seven o'clock, and we departed the Levies Station to have breakfast at one of the local restaurants before hitting the highway. We weren't even sure where our destination was going to be for the day – we were no longer in charge of ourselves or our schedule.

Our breakfast today consisted of 'Parathas' (chapatis cooked with lots of Ghee, basically fried chapatis), along with Chaa (Tea). Our armed Levies Guards stood at the ready outside the restaurant, with the security locks off and fingers on their triggers.

The whole episode was a bit nerve-wracking and we gulped down our morning meal within minutes. I hoped that we would get used to being surrounded by the military men as we travelled. Soon we were riding a sedate speed behind the armed trucks. The continued sixty-to-eighty-kilometer speed was a lot slower than we were used to travelling, and I was aching to open up the throttle and feel the wind on my face. When we had passed into Pakistan the driving lane had also changed from right to left, but since there was no traffic on the road, we were allowed to ride on the right side for the first couple of kilometers as we accustomed ourselves to the rules of being led.

There were check stops about every 50 kilometers, so the going was slow, as we were required to stop at each one and register. At each stop a uniformed man would come out to meet us, carrying a thick, handwritten logbook of all the foreigners that had passed that way. I was familiar with this procedure, as I had read a lot about it when doing my research for the trip, so we had all of our information handily printed on paper and provided a copy to each stop as we went along.

It was interesting to see that our escort vehicle and guards were being changed out at almost every stop as well. We found the Levies guards to be friendly and, even with the slow-moving travel, we were having fun, joking around with the guards and enjoying the sedate travel. We were offered cold drinks and water at most checkpoints, which was a blessing in such a hot and dry climate.

The desert area that is the province of Balochistan often has gusty winds, which we experienced as we were riding. The high winds were constantly pushing our bikes sideways off the highway, and resulted in an even slower pace. After about three hours, we reached Nokkundi, which was only 125 kilometers from Taftan. The whole day had been spent travelling and yet it seemed as if we hadn't gotten very far.

We politely asked the guards if it was possible for us to visit the Gurdwara Sahib, which they refused, stating that we were only allowed to go to our designated destinations. I was disappointed, but understood why we couldn't go.

Shortly after we passed Nokkundi, we informed our protectors that we would need to stop soon to fuel our bikes. After a few minutes they pulled over into a place that didn't look as if it offered fuel, but we were assured that we would receive good quality petrol, which is stored in drums instead of the standard pumps. The guards took it upon themselves to fill our fuel tanks up, and we were once again on our way. The check stops were continuing and, while thankful for each opportunity to stop and drink water in the heat, all the stopping and starting was starting to become tedious. After hours of being on the road, we followed our escort truck off onto a side road and into a big, gated courtyard. We had no idea where we were, but were soon informed that we had arrived at the Hotel Al Dawood in Dalbandin, and this would be where we would spend the night.

The seven hours that we had ridden today had only brought us a total of 290 kilometers down the road. We were pretty beaten up from the wind, and drained from the constant stops and slow speed, but, despite everything, feeling in high spirits.

We dragged our personal belonging into our assigned rooms, which were on the second floor. I was still thirsty, so I returned to the front desk to see if there was somewhere I could purchase a cold drink. The receptionist pointed me in the direction of a shop, which was right outside the hotel by the main entrance. We might have seen it if we had entered through the main gate of the hotel when arriving, but we had entered through the back, so we had missed it. However, as I was about to step outside to make my way to the store, I was stopped by one of the guards, who told me I wasn't allowed to leave the hotel alone. I needed protection and he would go with me.

I was greeted in Punjabi, as the gentleman in the store took note of my turban. He welcomed me to his shop and asked who I was and what I was doing there. When I told him the story of how our little group had come to be there, he happily exclaimed that he was also a Sindhi Sikh and lived in Dalbandin along with several other Sikh families. I was thrilled to learn there was a Gurdwara Sahib in the town as well.

I explained that we were not allowed to leave the hotel, so he sent a message to the local Sikh community and, a bit later, we were joined at the hotel by a half a dozen men. They had tried to contact the local politicians and officers in the area to make it possible for us to visit the Gurdwara Sahib, but hadn't had any luck. Since it wasn't possible, they instead had brought us Langar. As we were enjoying our holy food, we were surprised by unknown armed man who informed us that we could indeed leave to visit the Gurdwara Sahib.

As we walked down to the lobby, a tall man greeted us and told us that his brother was a senator in Islamabad, and his private security team would be taking us for the visit. He told us that the idea of Sikhs being in town and not being able to visit the Gurdwara Sahib was a thought that he couldn't comprehend.

Our short trip was an incredible experience, as the roads were basically shut down as we travelled through. It was a surreal journey as we rode with this influential man, with armed guards hanging outside the Land Cruiser. It was as if we were in a movie, providing us with a reality that we had never dreamed of.

Upon reaching the Gurdwara Sahib, we thanked everyone who had made this possible. Our gratefulness to the Sikhs of Dalbandin, who worked to get the permission from local authorities for us to visit, was an overwhelming feeling that we couldn't express fully.

By this time, it was quite late at night, but a large number of the local Sikh community was present and waiting for us. We all were given home-made blankets as souvenirs, and while we all knew that space was very limited to carry anything else with us, we gratefully accepted them, and I know that I will cherish mine for the rest of my life.

When we finally returned to the Hotel Al Dawood, it was almost midnight. Even more militia had arrived at the hotel and guards were posted outside each of our doors as we retired for the night. It was not easy to fall asleep, as we each tried to absorb all the things that we had experienced since we had departed from Taftan that morning.

MAY 3rd, 2019
FRIDAY

It was an early wake up for me, as it was only six in the morning when I rose from my bed. I took the opportunity to try to refresh myself by throwing some tepid water on myself, using the cup that was floating in the bucket that I had filled from the tap in the washroom. Without wasting any more time, I woke Jasmeet Singh and asked him to get ready as quickly as possible, as we had a long day of riding ahead of us. We planned to leave at eight o'clock with the Levies Officers.

By the time I had tied on my turban, the thoughtful local Sikhs had arrived with breakfast for us. We all gathered together to eat, and took the opportunity to spend a bit more time with the caring people who had come to see us off.

Our escort was waiting for us when we walked out into the courtyard, after pulling on our riding gear and grabbing our belongings. Our motorcycles were all set to ride, and we were interested to see what Waheguru had for us. The Levies Officers were pleased that we were ready on time and departed as scheduled. Within a few moments, we were happily perched on our bikes and out of the little town of Dalbandin, riding towards Quetta. The now customary frequent stops and changing of escorts, along with the slow speed didn't seem to bother us as much as it had previously.

It was a one-of-a-kind ride through the mountainous area of the country. As we travelled through one area particularly close to the Afghanistan border, one of the armed officers informed us that it was a dangerous zone to be in. I noticed that his trigger finger was at the ready and the safety of his gun was off. The tension was palpable, and as I followed and watched the officers, I couldn't imagine having their jobs.

The checkpoints allowed us to have a bit of relaxation time along the route, and proved to be a good way for us to be able to stretch and refresh ourselves. We rode for almost eight hours before passing through a tunnel to the view of the beautiful city of Quetta. Quetta has just over a million inhabitants, and is the only high-altitude city in Pakistan. It is known as the fruit city, as there are numerous orchards in the area.

We were asked to pull over before arriving into the city, and waited for about a half an hour before another vehicle and yet more uniformed men arrived. These armed men were travelling in what looked to be a bullet proof vehicle, the same kind as SWAT teams use in the western world.

It was an impressive motorcade as we had three escort vehicles, with their emergency lights on, and ourselves following on our motorcycles. We made our way through the narrow, busy roads of the city. The roads were exceptionally slippery, and it was a difficult ride for those of us on two wheels. Even with concentrating on keeping the bikes upright and moving forward, one of our team members had his machine slide out from under him when the vehicle in front of him came to a sudden stop. Luckily, he was not injured and before anyone else could take notice, several of the men in one of the escort vehicles jumped out and picked up the bike for him. After about a half hour of struggling with the roadways, we came upon a big metal gate, which opened upon our arrival, and closed and locked behind us. The sound of the gate slamming and locking behind us was intimidating and made me think of a prison.

We had reached our destination of the Hotel Bloom Star in Quetta. While we were busy checking in, we were told that this would be where we would be staying until we had permission to continue our travels. We would be provided guards by the local police service and we were not to leave the hotel on our own. I had been correct in my observation; this hotel was indeed our prison for the time being.

Reportedly, this hotel was the only one that would accept foreigners, and we tried to settle down into our rooms, but we were all concerned. We had been told that it could take two days to get permission to leave the city, and during that time we would have to stay in the hotel. At least the hotel had a courtyard where we could spend some time outside, we told each other, trying to find a good point in the situation.

We had a long day, riding in hot weather, and I was feeling the effects of the ride. I decided that an early night was in store for me, and headed to bed to try to rest.

MAY 4th, 2019
SATURDAY

I couldn't believe my eyes when I checked my phone to see what time it was. It was already ten in the morning, and I had slept longer than I had planned to. I had woken up with a high fever in the night and I was still feeling the heat of it pulsing through my body. While normally I didn't take any medications, I had popped a couple of Tylenol to help myself feel better.

After going through my morning routine, I went out to see if I could find the rest of the group. They were all sitting in the courtyard in their shorts, chatting and passing the time. Seeing them relaxing like this, I wasn't at all shocked to learn that we weren't leaving anytime soon. They kindly inquired about my state of health, but I had decided that I wasn't going to be completely honest with them, as I didn't want them to worry. I sat with them for a couple of minutes before heading to the front desk to see if I could get something from the kitchen to eat. My request was simply for a couple of slices of bread and some tea and I was grateful when the staff presented me with my request.

The day passed quietly. A Quetta-based Sikh and local leader, Jasvir Singh Khalsa, joined us at the hotel for lunch and to see how we were getting on. We spoke about the situation and the condition of living for Sikhs in the state of Balochistan. He explained that people of all religions in the country got along very well, and even the Sikhs, who were a minority in Pakistan, were doing fine. He also told us that he was certain that we wouldn't be allowed to leave the hotel to visit the local Gurdwara Sahib, but that he would try his best to make it happen.

Incredibly, after contacting the authorities, Jasvir Singh Khalsa managed to get permission for a motorcade for us to go around the city. I chose to stay back, due to not feeling well, but everyone else went for a quick trip. It was a hot day, and I wanted to save my strength for the rest of the journey. Riding a motorcycle when you are not feeling well is not a fun thing to do.

Jasvir Singh Khalsa, along with some of the other local Sikhs, showered rose petals to show respect and welcome the presence of local media along with the other members of our group. It was an incredible opportunity to have some interviews, which were played at later dates on the local television stations.

He also arranged a visit to the local Gurdwara later in the evening. I decided to join the rest of the group for this visit, even though I was still not well, as I didn't want to miss the chance to go. By that time of the day the heat had lessened and the slightly cooler temperature made me feel better. We were asked to hop into an unmarked car, which was surrounded by armed men riding in SUV's and on motorcycles.

Wide eyed stares followed us everywhere. The organized chaos of travelling through the streets was amazing, as each vehicle tried to out-honk each other and the men flashed their pistols and AK-47's, fingers and guns all at the ready.

There were a large number of Sikhs present in the Gurdwara Sahib. We were able to witness the infinite love of Sikhs for Guru Nanak. It was amazing to be greeted and wished luck by so many people. Jatinder Singh addressed the gathering, representing the group, and shared the information about who we were, what we were doing and where we were heading to, along with the appreciation that we felt for everyone who came out to meet us.

Through everything, the armed men in uniform followed us like shadows; always present, but thankfully never in our faces. It was ten thirty in the evening when we returned to our hotel prison; it had been a very nice break from being stuck in one place. It had been a strange sort of day, and I gratefully fell into bed again, with the air conditioning blowing full blast, to try to sleep off the effects of my illness. I just wanted to get well before we had to get back on the road.

MAY 5th, 2019
SUNDAY

We hadn't heard a word from our security detail about a potential departure, so we all decided to take it easy for another day and sleep in. I was making the most of our down time by resting as much as I could. I couldn't remember the last time I had fallen sick or had a fever such as this. Even when I am sick, I try to make it through without using any medications, but this was a different situation, so I had been taking Tylenol and spending as much time in bed as I could.

Jatinder Singh, Sukhvir Singh and Mandeep Singh came to see how I was faring and to ask me to dress and come down to the lobby area, where some of the local Sikh community were going to join us. By the time I readied myself, there were already a few families in the lobby conversing amongst themselves and the rest of the group. It was nice to sit and chat about a variety of things, including what life was like for them in Pakistan.

They were all very interested in knowing how we had gotten started on this journey and everything that had taken place since we started, and we all pitched in to regale them with our stories up until then. They had brought a huge banner with a welcome note from them to us, which made us feel very special. Once again, we found it difficult to show our appreciation for everything, as everyone had been so welcoming and kind. We could only hope that our words of thanks and gestures conveyed how we felt.

It was a nice visit, but once they left, we were left at odds of how to pass the rest of the day. It was an easy decision to wash and clean our motorcycles. Dust had collected on them while we travelled the past 730 kilometers in Pakistan and it was the perfect time to shine them up. A couple of young Balochi boys came to join us to wash and clean all of the bikes, which was fun.

I washed the chain of my motorcycle to remove the sand, then lubricated it again to make sure everything would run smoothly. I also emptied both sides of my TUSK panniers, the tank bag and the top box, since I hadn't had a chance to do this since we had departed Austria. I finished sorting my belongings and repacked them, remembering to put the thicker, warmer clothes at the bottom, as I definitely wouldn't be requiring them for the remainder of our historic ride.

We spent a bit of time speaking with the policemen who were guarding us, as they were friendly and curious about our lives in Canada and why we had chosen to take this trip. One of the armed men on duty told me that Balochistan is a smorgasbord of danger. There are Taliban leaders based in the capital of Quetta, and it is also the main route for drug smugglers running heroin and opium out of Afghanistan, not to mention the warring tribes of the native Baluchi people. Multiple buses had recently been bombed, and it was well known that the drug smugglers had occasionally kidnapped foreigners to use as leverage when dealing with police.

Later in the day we received welcome news when the head of our security force called to say that we had been given permission to leave the next morning at five o'clock. This was the news that we had all been waiting for. I was ecstatic that we were finally going to be on our way, but I was still feeling the effects of my illness and was wishing that I could feel full of energy for the next chapter of our journey. The peak of excitement was still to come – crossing the Wahga border and heading to Darbar Sahib Amritsar.

It was a treat, later in the evening, to see the eye-catching motorcycles of the bikers of Quetta when they came to visit us. Despite the chance to spend a bit more time chatting with them, as the rest of the group chose to, I headed back to my room to get what rest I could before our extremely early departure time the next day. It was important that we be ready and waiting for the security detail at the appropriate time.

MAY 6th, 2019
MONDAY

My alarm blared at four in the morning, and I quickly hit the snooze button before it could wake my roommate. I quickly rose and made my way to the bathroom to get ready for the day. It only took me twenty minutes to finish my morning routine and I was pleased to see that Jasmeet Singh was up when I came out. Before he could even ask the question, I told him that I was feeling much better. I finished preparing myself by tying on my black Dumala, pulling on the heavy riding gear, and grabbing my bag, which I slung across my shoulder. By the time I got down to where the bikes were parked, there was a team of uniformed men waiting for us, with their ever-present AK-47's.

The rest of the group joined me in loading our belongings back onto our machines and it didn't take us long to complete the task. As we were doing this, however, there was a young man, maybe in his teens, who was wiping down the windshields of our bikes. Jatinder Singh explained that the teenager had asked if he could speak to him before we left. We both thought that perhaps he was going to ask for money for cleaning the bikes.

It was a surprise to us when we asked him what he wanted and he replied, "Sidhu Saab ko mera Salaam kehna." (Pay my kind regards to Mr. Sidhu.) He wanted us to deliver this message to the Indian politician, Mr. Navjot Singh Sidhu, from the province of Punjab, who was advocating for better relations between India and Pakistan. He was much appreciated by the people of Punjab, on both sides, and other peace-loving people from India and Pakistan. While I do not support any politician, I found the exchange interesting as it tells everyone that a common man can be on either side of the border, in India or Pakistan, and just be someone who is against violence.

With his message ringing in our heads and our saddlebags packed, all we had to do was straddle our iron horses and signal the armed escort that we were ready to leave. The big metal gate creaked open as soon as we gave the thumbs up. There was another escort vehicle waiting outside the gate for us, waiting to become part of our convoy. It was an interesting, slightly empowering feeling to be rolling through the city streets with such a force with us. It came to mind that this might be what it felt like to be a mafia boss, with hired muscle to protect us from the masses. Even in this dangerous situation, it was fun to dream of movie-like scenarios.

The idea was to reach the city of Multan, located 830 kilometers from Quetta. Our Google maps was showing it as a twelve-hour drive and I wasn't sure if it would end up being longer or shorter than that. It was a pleasant morning as we headed through big mountains and craggy rocks. As soon as we were out of the city, most of our extra security forces stopped or fell behind, leaving just one lone vehicle to travel with us. It was a crazy procession of guards and vehicles, as every few kilometers the vehicle accompanying us would pull off and another would join us. At one point, there were two men on a 100cc motorcycle instead of a bigger vehicle. One man drove and the other sat behind him holding, not only his own gun, but the gun of the driver as well.

The sun was getting brighter and hotter, and by noon it was already forty five degrees Celsius. I couldn't tell if I still had a bit of a fever or if it was just the general heat that was overwarming me. Dehydration was a concern, so we kept drinking as much water as we could. Our first major stop was after the noon hour, when we stopped at the Gurdwara Sahib in a small town called Dera Murad Jamali. We had travelled about 270 kilometers since we had left Quetta, but it had taken us more than six hours with all the changing of guards. We spoke with the Sangat and made them aware of the services that Khalsa Aid provided internationally.

I was so hot and thirsty that, while everyone was talking to the locals, I downed three cans of chilled juice. We were blessed when we met the Sangat of the next village, Dera Allah Yar, which was just 30 kilometers down the road, at the bypass, as there was lunch waiting for us. We had received an incredible amount of love and support from the local Sikhs that it touched our hearts. After having lunch, we snuck in a power nap, which refreshed us from the heat of the sun and the length of the journey.

After Ardaas (prayer), we were back on the highway and once again following our escort. It was already three in the afternoon and I was getting a little impatient at the slowness of our travel. At one point our escort vehicle made a U-turn, assuming that the next vehicle would be in place and we would follow them. We waited for a few minutes, but the next shift never showed up. I wondered out loud why we were waiting, since we were feeling safe and the guards were slowing us down. The group agreed that we shouldn't waste any more time sitting and waiting, so we decided to try to make up some of the time we had lost with all the stops. We had only travelled about 220 kilometers since lunch and our nap, and it was already nine in the evening. We had only reached Daharki, Sindh, and there was still 300 kilometers to go before arriving at Multan, Punjab, where we had wanted to end the day.

It would be impossible to continue riding that distance though, which meant that we had to make other plans on the fly. The decision was made to stop for the night at Daharki. Sardar Tara Singh, the president of the Pakistan Shromani Committee, met us at the Gurdwara Baba Nanak Shah and explained that this Gurdwara Sahib is the central unit of the Sikh community in the state of Sindh, Pakistan. It is a one of a kind building in this town and amazing to view. We were grateful to have dinner at Gurdwara Sahib before settling down for a good night's sleep in an air-conditioned room. It was a great relief to have the cold air blowing on us after a long day of riding in the hot weather.

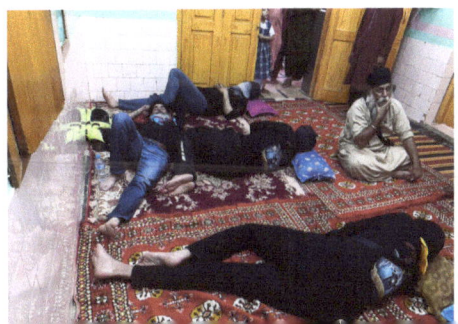

MAY 7th, 2019
TUESDAY

One of the many things that I had learned during this adventure was that a sound sleep and decent rest time is much needed with the type of travel that we were undertaking. Even though we hadn't had very many hours of sleep in Daharki, the decent mattresses that were provided and the air-conditioning created a relaxing atmosphere that gave us enough rest to refresh us.

We rose early and washed, feeling better than we had when we arrived the night previous. We took blessing from Gurdwara Nanak Shah, and donned our riding gear once again. Being accustomed to carrying our own gear, we were all surprised when the locals forcibly took our things from us and carried them the short distance to where our bikes were parked.

The Gurdwara Sahib management had also packed some Parathas (Chapatis cooked with lots of ghee) for us for lunch, since it was the first day of the month of Ramadan (fasting as per the Muslim religion, among other things). Most of the restaurants stay closed during this time since the majority of the population is Muslim, and Muslims don't eat from dawn until sunset during Ramadan.

It was still early when we departed, only six in the morning, and the first rays of sun were just peeking out. Our destination for the day was Nankana Sahib, Punjab, which was over 600 kilometers from where we were. I knew that even though it was a relatively short distance, it could potentially take us all day with stops and weather conditions.

Only about an hour passed, when approximately 50 kilometers down the road our road captains Azad Singh and Jatinder Singh pulled to the side of the road. Curious as to why they had stopped so soon after leaving, the question was answered when we viewed the sign that said "Welcome to Punjab". This was the border between the provinces of Sindh and Punjab.

This was a significant landmark for me. I drove as close as I could to the sign so that both myself and my bike could be captured in a photo that would remind me of this moment for the rest of my life. I was overcome with emotion, as for me, I feel that being Punjabi is, in a sense, belonging to two different, yet still significant, provinces, one on each side of the border of Pakistan and India. This area was once a country in itself, named Sarkar-e-Khalsa (Sikh Homeland or Sikh Raj). It had been ruled by the Maharaja Ranjit Singh, who was an exceptional leader and had recently been selected as best administrator to date in one of the surveys conducted by the BBC.

The province of Punjab in Pakistan is second largest province, and the most populated state of the country. It was originally the state of Punjab, which was divided during 1947, when India and Pakistan received their official independence from the British administration. As we were riding, we could see that the previously barren land was turning into golden wheat fields and arable farmlands. If one needed to compare the state of Punjab to somewhere else, I would think that it would be California, with the same kind of landscape and fertile fields. The air was filled with grain dust produced by the harvesting and handling of the wheat crops around us.

We drove until midday, which was about our halfway point for the day, before we stopped for a significant break. We found a little local Dhaba (roadside restaurant) where we could eat the food that we had brought with us without having to order and disturbing the fast of Ramadan. We were thankful that the owner was willing to provide us with some tea.

The hot sun was beating relentlessly down, and the decision was made to stay off the road for a couple of hours, as the heat was so intense. We took the opportunity to have a short nap and rest ourselves, as we knew that we would probably have a lot of activity upon arriving at our final destination today.

Consulting our Google Maps app, we looked for the shortest route to Nankana Sahib, which was where we wanted to get to by the end of the day. I was intrigued to see that Google Maps showed us that the route would take us on the new M3 motorway, which had just opened the month prior, and connected Multan to Lahore. We straddled our beasts once again and headed out.

It was mid-afternoon and it was hot. The air rushing by our faces gave us no relief and I was sweltering in my heavy riding gear. We were not quite at the M3, travelling on the side roads, when we came across an irresistible opportunity to cool ourselves down. There was a tube well pumping water for the fields, and in no time we were soaking ourselves, fully clothed, in the slightly cooler water. It was a reminder of my younger years, as I hadn't done anything like this for a long time.

Laughing and joking, we got back on the bikes to continue, and, it seemed within minutes I was completely dry again. We continued on, only stopping for a moment to ask a local cyclist if we were on the right route to get to the main highway. We were delighted when he said that he had seen us on television a few days earlier, being interviewed during our stay in Quetta.

We reached the M3 and realized quickly that it was probably one of the best highways that we had come across yet. There was a snag in our plan to use the motorway though, as we discovered when we were stopped at one of the check points. Motorcycles are not allowed on any motorways in Pakistan. We explained to the officer that our Google Maps had brought us here as the shortest route, and, upon learning that we were on a ride from Canada to Amritsar, he kindly let us proceed, but not before taking a selfie with us first. We were happy to hear this, as taking the side roads would have slowed us down considerably.

The ride continued on the elevated highway, which didn't have much traffic at all. At one point, I was moved to tears as I saw a sign saying, "Toba Tek Singh", which is a Sikh name. I felt so connected to everything at that moment that my throat choked up and I had a hard time continuing to focus on the road as I wiped my streaming tears away.

As I was trying to absorb my feelings and trying to soak in every aspect of the ride, we were pulled over by the highway patrol. My heart sunk as we parked and they came over to speak with us. We were only about an hour away from Nankana Sahib, and it was already six in the evening. If we needed to travel on the side roads it would take us much longer to arrive and we knew that there were people waiting for us. They informed us that they had received a call from Lahore, the capital of Punjab, about some motorcycles riding on the motorway, and that we were to be stopped.

While the highway patrol officers were very polite about the situation, they still had to do their jobs, which was to request that we follow them and leave the highway at the next exit. We complied, following them to a small local store where we were served chilled watermelon, which had been set aside for eating after sunset.

We had to wait until the senior officer arrived, which wasn't until eight in the evening. It was already dark and we were impatient to get going. Mr. Bhatti, the senior officer, explained that a couple of officers would be escorting us on the side roads to get to Nankana Sahib. Just as we were getting ready to depart, he requested a photo with us, and after a moment's consideration, changed his mind about how we would travel. He told us that we could, in fact, travel on the motorway, with the officers accompanying us. When we asked if he was sure that was okay, he told us that he would deal with the higher authorities later.

We felt as if we had received a miracle. We thanked Guru Nanak for the blessing and departed. The highway patrol stayed behind us while we travelled, but moved to the front of the group when we were about to exit for Nankana Sahib.

It was ten at night by the time we reached our stop for the night. There were a lot of local Sikhs present and waiting for us. We were welcomed by the chant of "Bole So Nihal" Jaikaras and were showered with rose petals as we arrived. Garlands of flowers were given to us to wear. My heart swelled as uncontrollable emotions threatened to well up inside me again. Nankana Sahib is the birth place of Guru Nanak, the first master of Sikhs, and is someplace that every Sikh wants to visit.

Arrangements had been made for us to stay in the guest rooms here, so after unloading the bikes and taking a quick shower, we sat down with Lovely Singh aka Bhupinder Singh, who we had met upon reaching Nankana Sahib Gurdwara Sahib.

He had live telecasted our arrival on the Punjabi Lehar YouTube Channel, which he and his partner Nasir Dhillon run. Punjabi Lehar is well known among Punjabis around the globe for its content. Lovely Singh offered his services to provide the live coverage of our activities in Pakistan, to which we gladly agreed. He also asked us about the places we wanted to visit before we head out to Amritsar, our final destination, so that he could plan accordingly.

It was well past midnight when we went to bed. It had been a long day but one of the most blessed days of the ride, and possibly even our lives.

MAY 8th, 2019
WEDNESDAY

I slept in, due to the lateness of the hour from the evening before, and partly because I wanted to rest as much as possible, as I was still concerned a little about my health. There were only a few days before we would reach Amritsar, which was our final stop on this journey. Everyone else was already up and prepared for the day though, so I hurried to get myself ready.

The idea of being at this location had been on our minds since the very first day, and today it was becoming a reality. We entered through a massive, golden, main door which was carved meticulously with sacred symbols and the depictions of various Sikh leaders who had fought courageously in Saka Nankana. Everything to do with this visit was bringing up emotions in all of us.

The Gurdwara committee presented us with 'Siropas'. A siropa is a piece of cloth, which is about two meters in length, given to one to show recognition of one's contribution towards the community. Bhai Sahib Rajvir Singh took us inside the main building and narrated the story of when Guru Nanak came into the world on April 15th, 1469.

We saw the bullet holes inside the main Darbar, which have been preserved to remind all of the Saka Nankana Sahib which took place in February, 1921. Saka Nankana Sahib forms a very important part of Sikh history and, in political significance, it comes next only to the Jallianwala Bagh massacre of April, 1919. The saka constitutes the core of the Gurdwara Reform Movement started by the Sikhs in early twentieth century. The interesting part of this saka (demonstration or agitation) is the unprecedented discipline, self-control and exemplary patience displayed by the peaceful Sikh protesters even in the face of extreme barbarism.

On the same premises, we saw a Jand tree which stands where Sardar Lachhman Singh was tied and burnt alive. He attained martyrdom on February 21, 1921, during the period of time when the buildings were returned to the Sikhs.

After having Langar at Gurdwara Sahib, we went along with Lovely Singh to meet the D.C. of Nankana Sahib, at his invitation. It was within walking distance, so we had no reason to get out the bikes and instead took the opportunity to stretch our legs. Upon meeting with the Deputy Commissioner, we requested if it would be possible that the road outside the Gurdwara Sahib be improved, as there would be many visitors coming from everywhere in the world in the next few months to celebrate the 550th anniversary of Guru Nanak's birthday. After our meeting, we left for Gurdwara Sacha Sauda, which was about 45 kilometers away, accompanied by Lovely Singh and Nasir Dhillon. This is where Guru Nanak Dev Ji started the concept of Langar (free food for all). The langar serves only vegetarian food in order to make it inclusive of all faiths. To date, the Sikh community worldwide is continuing with that tradition of providing free food at every Gurdwara. "Wandd Shakko" (share what you have), is one of the three main concepts of Sikhism and free food is a perfect example of it.

We had tea and snacks at Gurdwara Sacha Sauda, before leaving for Gurdwara Panja Sahib, our final destination of the day. Gurdwara Panja Sahib is located in Hassan Abdal, which is about 350 kilometers from Gurdwara Sacha Sauda. I was travelling with Lovely Singh in his car and was very much enjoying his company and the conversation. We were travelling on the M-2 motorway, going to Islamabad, and discovered that it was yet another fantastic highway. One moment during the trip will always stand out in my mind. We pulled up to a toll plaza and the barrier dropped in front of us, indicating that we had to stop and pay. As soon as Lovely Singh unrolled his window, however, the attendant said that if he had realized that he was a Sikh he would have let him pass through with no charge. Unfortunately, since the barrier was down, now he had to pay.

This was such a great example of how Sikhs are respected in Pakistan, contrary to the belief of most people outside of Pakistan, Lovely Singh explained how this happened to him now and again, bringing up a feeling of pride for our people and much respect for Pakistan.

We took the time to stop at one of the exits for dinner, encountering some of the leading fast-food restaurants from around the world. Due to our slightly later departure and the stop for dinner, it was late at night by the time we arrived at Panja Sahib. It didn't seem to matter that we were late though, as the Gurdwara Sahib management was waiting to welcome us and to listen to the message of our mission.

Our host, Lovely Singh and Nasir Dhillon insisted that we stay awake awhile longer and spend some time sitting beside the holy water pool of Gurdwara Sahib. The atmosphere of purity, with the whispers of flowing water, helped us to overcome our tiredness of the month-long riding. Pakistan is incredibly rich in Sikh history and heritage, which is the main reason for the Sikhs from all over the world to visit, and we felt blessed that we had the opportunity to be here.

When we were done soaking up the ambience for the evening, we retired to the guest house of the Gurdwara Panja Sahib, which is part of the main premises and where we would be sleeping. As long as the day had been, I took a moment to be grateful before closing my eyes into blissful sleep.

MAY 9th, 2019
THURSDAY

It was such a blessing to be part of the morning prayers at Gurdwara Panja Sahib. Once again, we were given siropas from the administration during the ceremony and introduced to the gathering with some information about our ride and fundraising. The time here provided us with an incredible opportunity to not only see the sacred rock with Guru Nanak's handprint, but also be able to bathe ourselves with the pure, holy water that had been flowing endlessly from beneath the rock since the day Guru Nanak touched it.

The legend of this spring and pool is famous and dates back to 1521 CE (1578 B.K.), when Guru Nanak, along with Bhai Mardana reached Hassan Abdal in Baisakh Samwat. The story tells us that in the shade of a tree, Guru Nanak and Bhai Mardana recited Kirtan, while their devotees gathered around them. This annoyed a local saint, called Shah Wali Qandhari. Needing to quench his thirst, Guru Nanak sent Bhai Mardana three times to ask Shah Wali Qandhari for water, which he refused each time. Despite the rude replies, Mardana continued asking politely. The Wali asked, *"Why don't you ask your Master whom you serve?"* Mardana Ji went back to the Guru in a miserable state and exclaimed, *"Oh lord! I prefer death to thirst and will not approach Wali the egoist again."* The Guru replied, *"Oh Bhai Mardana ji! Repeat the Name of God, the Almighty; and drink the water to your heart's content."* The Guru pulled aside a big rock and a pure fountain of water sprang up and began to flow endlessly. Bhai Mardana quenched his thirst and felt grateful to the Guru. Soon after, the fountain of Shah Wali Qandhari dried up, and witnessing this, the Wali, in his rage threw a part of a mountain towards the Guru from the top of the hill. The Guru stopped the hurled rock with his hand, leaving an imprint of a right hand on it. Observing the miracle, Wali became the Guru's devote.

The Gurdwara was named Panja Sahib by Hari Singh Nalwa, the most famous general of the Sarkar-e-Khalsa (Sikh Empire) and he is credited with having built the first Gurdwara at this sacred site. We enjoyed breakfast in the Langar hall within Gurdwara Sahib before leaving for Gurdwara Darbar Sahib Kartarpur also known as Kartarpur Sahib. Located in Shakargarh, in the Narowal District of the Punjab province, Kartarpur Sahib was 470 kilometres away, which we estimated to be about a six-hour ride. It was a long ride, but worth enough to see the land where Guru Nanak Dev Ji had spent a few final years of his life sharing the message of 'Kirat Karo' (earn a living) to everyone. Along the route, I learned an interesting fact from Lovely Singh about our initial arrival. He explained that the main gate of the Gurdwara Janam Asthan Nankana Sahib always stayed close, except for one day a year when there is a parade for Guru Nanak Dev Ji's birthday. On that day, the vehicle carrying Guru Granth Sahib enters and exits through the big gate. I was surprised to learn this, as the gate had been opened for us to arrive on our motorcycles. This was a huge blessing for us and something that we had never expected.

It was about three in the afternoon by the time we reached Kartarpur Sahib. The moment our feet hit the ground we were all overwhelmed by the thought that we were touching the very soil that Guru Nanak Dev Ji had once ploughed, watered and harvested. This is a very sacred spot for the Sikh people, but because it was located on Pakistani land, our people had requested both governments to allow a corridor that would provide pilgrims an opportunity to visit this sacred site.

It was nice to witness the construction that was taking place to put the corridor in place, and we learned that the work was being done as quickly as possible, in order to have it ready for November, only six months in the future. Having it completed by then would allow any pilgrims to visit on the 550th birth anniversary of Guru Nanak Dev Ji. We listened to the narration of the history and the explanation of the Kartarpur Corridor by Sardar Inder Singh, the caretaker of Gurdwara Sahib. After our little tour and information session, we were extremely blessed to have Langar made from the crops which came from Guru Nanak's own fields. I had never tasted anything as divine as the lentils, vegetables and wheat products that we were served. The serenity, along with the presence of Baba Nanak in the forests and farms by the River Ravi makes this a unique place. The quiet premises, disturbed only by the chirping of birds, made the opportunity to enjoy the organic Langar, served in the open yard, a once in a lifetime experience. I had never felt quite so blessed.

What will remain in my memory though, is a conversation with a Muslim man who was helping to serve Langar. The caretaker had explained that this man had lost his farmland when the government had acquired what was needed to build the Corridor. Even though he had been paid for the land, we couldn't imagine how he felt about it, but when Mandeep Singh, one of our riders, asked him how he felt about the transaction, he graciously replied that he thought that he had been blessed to have his land be part of Baba Nanak's home. It brought up the realization that people from all backgrounds and other religions also revered Guru Nanak and his teachings.

After Langar, Inder Singh took us to the border which separated the two Punjabs, and showed us the entire development of the Corridor, which was impressive. I was stunned that they could complete all the work required before November.

Later in the day, we drove back to Gurdwara Janam Asthan Nankana Sahib to stay for another night before heading out for Lahore the next morning.

MAY 10th, 2019
FRIDAY

It was necessary to rise a bit earlier today, so I hit the button to turn off my alarm before making my way to the washroom to get ready. We all wanted to make the best use of our time here, and this was our last day before crossing over the Wagah border on our way to Darbar Sahib Amritsar, our final destination of this incredible journey. As I made my way to the prayer hall, I couldn't believe that our trip was almost over. It had seemed so long in planning, and yet the travel days had gone by so quickly.

It was another divine morning as we visited the birthplace of Guru Nanak once more before partaking of Langar. We were headed out to Lahore, which was about 80 kilometers away. Our GPS was showing this to be about an hour's drive, but our escort was so slow that it turned into about two hours on the road.

Lovely Singh and Nasir Dhillon from the Punjabi Lehar Channel travelled beside the motorcade with their crew to film the whole journey. It was really hot, but we were feeling fine on the motorcycles, not to mention the excitement of approaching our destination was keeping our minds on other things.

We headed straight out to our first stop in Lahore, which was the Evacuee Trust Property Board Office which administers evacuee properties, including educational, charitable or religious trusts left behind by Hindus and Sikhs who migrated after partition. They welcomed us and presented us with souvenirs to remind us of our visit.

We parked our bikes at Gurdwara Dehra Sahib and dropped our belongings in the room provided by the administration. In 1606, the fifth Sikh Guru, Arjan Dev was martyred here. The famous and revered Gurdwara is part of an ensemble of monuments which includes the Lahore Fort, Samadhi of Ranjit Singh, Huzoori Bagh, Roshnai Gate, and the Badshahi Mosque. While one is entering the fort, one can see the beauty of the Dera Sahib and the Gurdwara. This monument is a best example of Sikh Architecture and reflects the values of tolerance, wonderful intricacy, magnificence and line work. It is no wonder that Sikh pilgrims from all over the world want to visit.

Right beside the Gurdwara is the Royal Fort where Sarkar-e-Khalsa's (Sikh Empire) flag flew for almost 50 years. The Darbar Hall of Maharaja Ranjit Singh, along with the Maharani Jind Kaur's bedroom are all evidence of our rich and royal heritage. We also took a couple of minutes to visit the Samadhi of Maharaja Ranjit Singh, which is an 18th-century building in Lahore. This houses the funerary urns of the Sikh ruler Maharaja Ranjit Singh. One of the last places we wanted to visit was the museum where things related to the Sikh Empire were displayed, but when we arrived, we discovered that it had already closed for the day. When we spoke to the officers on duty, they called their superiors to see if anything could be done for us. After explaining who we were, they were authorized to cut the seal that was put at the entrance at the end of each day. The respect that we had for the authorities in Pakistan was beyond words, as we were continually shown such courtesy and kindness. We were told that the items belonged to Sikhs and all of us had a right to visit and see them.

We couldn't miss going to Badshahi Masjid, which is the second largest mosque in Pakistan. Here we met a lot of locals who were very interested in the ride we were doing. It was fun to take pictures with them and our motorcycles and I was reminded that no matter where we went, there were wonderful people to welcome us.

It was also an incredible thought to know that even though there was a border separating the land, that the general people still believe in one Punjab.

The day passed quickly and while we were enjoying all the visits and sites, we were also being bombarded with messages on social media about our schedule for the next day. We would be crossing the Wahga border and entering Punjab, before travelling on to Amritsar. All of the enquiries were being forwarded to Sarghi Kaur Barring, who had volunteered to host the meet and greet which had been organized after crossing the Wahga border. Motorcyclists from Punjab and other states were anxiously waiting to meet us and the last few days had definitely kept Sarghi very busy with organizing, along with dealing with the electronic and print media at both the national and local levels.

We had been invited by the Ravadari Society to share more about our ride, and we were happy to see that they were working to promote multiculturalism and the equal treatment of everyone. It was a wonderful chance to share our story and learn more about theirs. A stop in the Anarkali Bazaar treated us to some delicious local items, like lassi (buttermilk), gol-gappe, and fresh juice. There were some touching moments, when we tried to pay for our food and drinks and our money was refused. Everyone considered us their guests. It was hard for me, with my now more Western thinking, to accept this, but I was feeling incredibly blessed to be a Sikh and proud that the reason behind these gestures was because of how these people had been treated during the Sikh Empire. Along with our visits and activities, we had been invited to a ride through the busiest Mall Road of Lahore by the bikers of the Cross Route Club. We were welcomed in a unique way by the fifty or more bikers, with posters commemorating our visit, before they joined us for a ride. At the end, they treated us to ice cream and a chance to social with our biker brothers. Once again, we felt like royalty as we enjoyed the city and our companions.

It was quite late by the time we returned to our sleeping quarters, but despite the busy day and hot weather, which should have drained me, I had a hard time falling asleep. The thought of entering Punjab the next day was bringing up a feeling in me that was beyond words.

MAY 11th, 2019
SATURDAY

It was a big day today, the last of our long ride. Today was the day that we would live out the moment that we had been talking about since the beginning, the day we would enter the final country on our list. The very thought of entering my birth country, Punjab, made me overly emotional and I wasn't quite sure how to process everything that was bubbling up inside me.

I had goosebumps when I woke, from the excitement and anticipation of the upcoming day. I was feeling so refreshed and energetic, that even the idea of being in the hot sun all day wasn't bothering me. We had decided to match each other in our turban style today, along with our clothing, to blend aesthetically together as a team, so I dressed myself in a Kesari (saffron) Patialashai style turban, blue jeans, the black official t-shirt of the ride, and my Forma riding boots.

We departed from Gurdwara Dehra Sahib after a light breakfast and a prayer, towards the Punjab border, which was only about 30 kilometers away. It was exhilarating to travel the last few kilometers in Pakistan, knowing we would soon be over the border. Even though I had enjoyed the fantastic riding conditions on the highways here, along with the incredible generosity, respectfulness, and kindness of the people of Pakistan, I was still eagerly looking forward to the next phase of our journey

Lovely Singh and Nasir Dhillon joined us, along with their film crew, to see us off at the border. Even though it was a short distance, it still took us almost an hour to get to the border, where we were welcomed by the Pakistan officials, who took care of getting our passports and Carnets stamped.

Every border is different in their processes, but no matter the place, it seems as if more time is needed than we ever anticipate, and it was close to an hour before all the paperwork was completed for us to leave Pakistan. We were offered cold drinks while we were impatiently waiting, which was a nice gesture. Our phones were constantly ringing with calls from the other side of the border, by people wanting to know when we would be arriving. There were a lot of motorcyclists and media waiting for us.

We said our final goodbyes to the Punjabi Lehar team and started riding towards a large gate, just a few meters away from where we were. The gate opened and we were at our final destination – Punjab – where we all had been born and grown up. Emotions bubbled to the surface as we took in the significance of being home.

As soon as my wheels crossed the border, I rested my bike on its stand and knelt on the ground. Pressing both my hands and my forehead to the ground of my birth country, I showed my respect to this land that I had always been proud to be from, my Punjab, my birthplace. I had spent my childhood here, and completed my schooling here. It was only later in life, when I was looking for other opportunities, that I migrated to Canada, the land of possibilities.

We had done it! We had completed our mission, to ride from Canada to Punjab and the sudden feeling of accomplishment was overwhelming. We were welcomed with garlands of fresh flowers by SGPC (Shiromani Gurdwara Parbandhak Committee), along with Baba Sewa Singh and a few others who were accompanying them, before we were asked by the border security to head to immigration and customs to get our paperwork completed. Time flew as we chatted gaily with everyone around us, and it was half past two by the time we were cleared by customs and had our Carnets and passports stamped.

It was with an incredulous feeling that we met with some prominent members of our Sikh Motorcycle Club in Vancouver, who had flown over to meet us as we crossed the border. Sardar Jaspal Singh Bahga, Rachhpal Singh Dhaliwal, Amandeep Singh Garcha, and Gurpreet Singh Tung, had made the long flight to Punjab to greet us, along with Sarghi Kaur Barring, our media coordinator who had organized and coordinated all the media interaction throughout our time. Sarghi Kaur had been an amazing support throughout our ride, even taking time off work to help us with all the media coverage, and I couldn't express enough thanks to her.

I was extremely pleased to see our fellow motorcycle club members from home, and was once again overtaken with feelings as Amandeep Singh Garcha gave me a big hug and told me that he would forever regret that he hadn't been part of the ride, but that he was immensely proud that he was able to fly in to receive us at the border.

The first point of order was to take some celebratory photos. It was impossible to take pictures with everyone who was waiting, but we did the best we could in the short period of time that we had. There were press agents waiting to interview us and we still needed to get on the road to complete our trip. It was four in the afternoon by the time we finished with a press conference heralding our arrival.

We were scheduled to ride a short 30 kilometers down the road to Darbar Sahib Amritsar, which we had expected to take a short time, but were taken aback that there were over 200 motorcyclists from all over the country waiting to accompany us to our very final destination. The revving of the motors and sound of the many wheels on the pavement is something that will forever remain in my memory. There is no feeling quite like riding with such a large group.

Darbar Sahib, means "exalted court", or The Golden Temple, and is also known as Harmandir Sahib (adobe of God). It is the preeminent spiritual site of Sikhism. The gurdwara is built around a man-made pool that was completed by the fourth Sikh Guru, Guru Ram Das, in 1577. Guru Arjan Dev, the fifth Guru, requested Baba Sain Mir Mohammed Sahib, a famous Muslim Sufi saint of Lahore, to lay its foundation stone in 1589. In 1604, Guru Arjan placed a copy of the Guru Granth Sahib in Darbar Sahib. The Gurdwara was repeatedly rebuilt by the Sikhs after it became a target of persecution and was destroyed several times by the Mughal and invading Afghan armies. Maharaja Ranjit Singh, after founding the Sarkar-e-Khalsa (Sikh Empire), rebuilt it using marble and copper in 1809, and overlaid the sanctum with gold foil in 1830. This has led to the name the Golden Temple.

The Golden Temple is spiritually the most significant shrine in Sikhism, but is an open house of worship for all people from all walks of life and faiths. The complex is a collection of buildings around the sanctum and the pool, of which one of these is Akal

Takht, the chief center of religious authority of Sikhs. Over 100,000 people visit the holy shrine daily for worship.

Even though we were a lot later than expected, an astounding 2,000 people were waiting to greet us as we rode in one by one. The resounding sound of the chant of Bole So Nihal, Sat Sri Akal, created an air of excitement and joy that I had never experienced before. My heart filled with pride as I heard the words being chanted by so many people. This was more than I had ever expected.

It was about five in the afternoon by the time we finally reached Darbar Sahib and the moment came when we could park our bikes in front of the Ghanta Ghar (clock tower). Some of the members of the SGPC led us into the office and presented us with siropas, along with an antique picture of Darbar Sahib Amritsar. We were extremely blessed to be able to sit in the designated area and listen to the Shabad Kirtan. I was filled with thankfulness that our adventure had been successful, with no major problems or accidents. It was a moment to be cherished.

Our mission, and expedition, was over, but the memories of our time riding, the people we encountered, the generosity that we found, and the kindness of the locals in every country, would live on in our hearts and memories forever.

THE FINAL DAYS

Our general mission completed; our little group carried on with some of the formalities of finishing our ride from Canada to Punjab. We were invited to participate in another ride, a motorcycle rally that would take us, and about 550 other motorcyclists, from Khadur Sahib to Sultanpur Lodhi. It had been organized by Giani Narinder Singh, who is the administrator of the Gurdwara Dukh Niwaran Sahib in Surrey. He enlisted the help of Baba Sewa Singh, who is the Head of Kar Sewa Khadur Sahib, and runs institutes under his patronage through Nishan-e-Sikhi Charitable Trust. This was more of a Nagar Kirtan (Religious Sikh Parade) than anything else and we rode for approximately 35 kilometers with the rest of the bikers. Upon reaching Sultanpur Lodhi, a tree was planted for each of one of our members from Canada, and our names were put on them to commemorate our mission.

Another press meeting had been organized in Ludhiana, where I had the honor of meeting Bhai Daljit Singh Bittu. During the armed phase of Sikh struggle for freedom and Sikh Homeland, after the holocaust of June, 1984 and the Genocide of November, 1984, this man had played a major role. For me, the chance to meet him was exciting, and a key moment in our encounter for me was the opportunity to hug him. I still do not have the words to express my respect or feeling for this selfless human being who had sacrificed his present for the future of Sikh Nation.

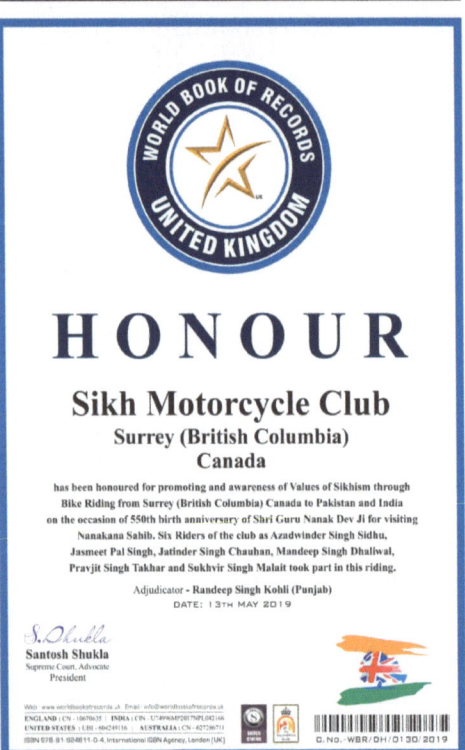

The last event that we attended was another occasion to tell our complete story and be able to secure even more donations for Khalsa Aid. This event had been organized by the Himalayan Harley Davidson, an authorized Harley Davidson dealership in Chandigarh for HOG members. It was a pleasure for us to present our story and receive some souvenirs from the members as well.

On May 13, 2019, we were incredibly elated to find out that the Sikh Motorcycle Club of Surrey had received an honorary certificate from the World Book of Records, United Kingdom, for promoting awareness of the values of Sikhism through Bike Riding from Canada to Punjab. After our duties were complete, our little group split up to ride to each one of our native villages and spend some personal time in the places of our origins. I was so proud to be able to ride to my village of Dherian, in the District of Jalandhar, where I was greeted by a large number of people at the local Gurdwara Sahib.

Through the remainder of my days in Punjab, I thought a lot about the places we had been and the people we had met, and even some of the amusing moments that had taken place both before and throughout the trip. While our true mission had been to raise funds for Khalsa Aid during this epic journey, there was a lot of fun and laughter that had taken place along the way, some had to do with misunderstandings of language, while others were comments about our undertaking.

I will forever chuckle when I think of an interview that Mandeep Dhaliwal was doing, when the woman interviewing him asked him if we had any issues with food during our travels. Mandeep replied that we had no problems with food or gas along the route.

Of course, he was referring to fuel or petrol, but used the Canadian version of that – gas. The interview was in Punjab, where the word gas means something completely different, causing everyone to burst into laughter. The young lady conducting the interview was embarrassed to say the least, thinking that Mandeep was referring to bodily functions rather than petrol, as he mentioned food and gas in the same sentence. A humorous moment that neither she, nor we, will soon forget.

I also remembered a comment that had been made by Mr. Thandi before we departed, when he mentioned that the whole thing was a crazy idea and that he was not crazy enough to join us for the trip. His congratulations at the end of the adventure were heartfelt though, when he told us how brave he thought we were for completing our mission. It made me consider the fact that people look at situations or things in a different way when it is proven that they can be done.

Of course, there were some final details to be taken care of, such as getting our motorcycles back to Canada, and we were blessed to have the help of our friend Gurlqbal Singh Gill for this task. The bikes were shipped the long way home by sea and they reached Canada in September, 2019. One of my final tasks for the bikes was to courier the stamped carnets of all six bikes to Sukie Duhaney at CARS (Classic Automotive Relocation Services) in England, and she reimbursed 2,250 pounds to each of us.

The original mission of raising money for Khalsa Aid had been a resounding success. Throughout our ride we had managed to raise an astounding $105,000.00 CDN for this noble cause. When I saw the final figure, my heart filled with pride.

I flew back to Canada on May 30th, as I needed to get back to work. I had taken two months off, and I couldn't thank my employer enough for letting me take extended vacation time to live out my dream. Travel exposes you to the most rewarding, and most heartbreaking parts of civilization, and I felt that I had been exposed to both aspects along the way.

I couldn't believe that after all the lengthy planning and anticipation, the time that we had spent on this special adventure was over so quickly, but I knew that I would be holding on to the special memories and the friendships that I had forged during this time for the rest of my life.

It doesn't matter who we become in life, or how successful we are, it will always feel good to return to the place we came from. I believe this was one of the reasons I was so excited and enthusiast about planning this ride, not to mention living it. I am not sure there would be any other ride that would provide me with as much joy or satisfaction as this one did. Canada to Punjab, an odyssey that I would never be able to repeat.

"A GOOD LIFE IS LIVED AS PART OF A COMMUNITY, BY LIVING HONESTLY AND CARING FOR OTHERS."

FROM THE AUTHOR

When you consider two very different parts of the world as home, it is difficult to describe how it feels as you travel from one to the other, and so the title of this book was born. To me, "Heading Home" describes not only the journey to my birth country of Punjab, but also the return to Canada, where my home has been since 1993. In my heart, I am a Sikh and Punjabi, while also wearing my Canadian citizenship with honour and pride. There does not need to be a distinction between the two. I carry my birth country's history and my beliefs as part of who I am, but can not express enough gratitude to the country of Canada for helping shape my life into what it is today.

Driving out into the world on the back of a motorcycle took me into many unknowns, and allowed me to see people, cultures and places in a different manner; forcing me to step out of my shell. In my wildest imagination, it would not have occurred to me to undertake an adventure such as this, and even beyond that, to then put the tale of that odyssey into the written word to spread the message to others. I am not a writer, nor a storyteller, and so this journey is still creating new opportunities for me years after it ended. With so many people around the world asking me to update them on what happened during our travels, and their belief in me to create a book, I decided to put my fingers to the keyboard and try to tell my story as best as possible.

What the future holds for me, I do not yet know. Perhaps there will be another chance to experience something like this, or perhaps not. In any case, I will be holding fast onto the memories of my travels forever, and I sincerely hope that you will enjoy reading about my motorcycle adventure with my friends and companions. Of course, I would love to hear your thoughts, and appreciate any feedback that readers want to share by email, or online comments.

Enjoy the journey!

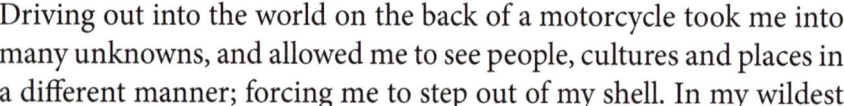

www.ingramcontent.com/pod-product-compliance
Lightning Source LLC
Chambersburg PA
CBHW041710160426
43209CB00018B/1790